MILITARY TRANSPORT

TRUCKS & TRANSPORTERS

GREENHILL MILITARY MANUALS

MILITARY TRANSPORT
TRUCKS & TRANSPORTERS

GREENHILL MILITARY MANUALS

T. J. O'MALLEY

ILLUSTRATED BY RAY HUTCHINS

Greenhill Books, London
Stackpole Books, Pennsylvania

Military Transport: Trucks and Transporters
first published 1995 by
Greenhill Books, Lionel Leventhal Limited, Park House
1, Russell Gardens, London NW11 9NN
and
Stackpole Books, 5067 Ritter Road, Mechanicsburg, PA 17055, USA

British Library Cataloguing in Publication Data
T.J. O'Malley
Military Transport: Trucks and Transporters - (Greenhill Military Manuals; No. 3)
I. Title II. Hutchins, Ray
III. Series 623.74
ISBN 1-85367-202-5

Library of Congress Cataloging in Publication Data
available

Typeset by Merlin Publications
Printed in Great Britain by The Bath Press, Avon

Introduction

No matter how they are named, as logistics vehicles, B vehicles, soft-skins, or whatever, load-carrying vehicles form the supporting sinew of any armed force.

Such vehicles are used to transport personnel and all the many and various supplies, stores and ammunition without which no modern armed force can survive, let alone fight.

Wherever armed forces are based or operate, the B vehicle is never far away. They may lack the 'glamour' of the armoured vehicles but load - carrying trucks and other similar vehicles are essential to the continued operation of any armed force.

The vehicles mentioned in this book come in many forms, from the little light runabouts used by airborne and special forces to the massive tank transporters that haul heavy loads over long distances.

The selection included in this book cannot be encyclopaedic and is only a small sample of the many models and types of load - carrying military vehicle that abound throughout the military world.

Some models and makes have had to be omitted simply for lack of space but the selection provided does give at least one example of just about every type of B vehicle in use today, together with a selection of their variants.

The variants are important because many basic chassis are often modified or converted for roles that seem to have little connection with the original role of load or personnel transport.

Many vehicles, such as the French ACMAT series, are produced in a bewildering array of variants, all based on one original design. In contrast some vehicles remain simply at the 'one type' stage.

The Future

At first sight there seems to be little enough to consider relating to the future of the truck. It has to be said that the trucks of today look little different in design terms from those of two or more decades back and few innovations seem possible. Yet things are changing. The nature of what the future will hold can be seen with the overall design concept of the American Family of Medium Tactical Vehicles (FMTV - qv) to which design modularity has been extensively applied to the extent that a high proportion of components are shared between the 2.5 and 5 ton versions, thereby offering considerable savings in spares holdings, maintenance costs, and so forth. There is also the selection of a modern 'lean burn' diesel engine coupled to an automatic transmission, which not only offers high fuel efficiency but is coupled with low harmful exhaust emissions. The latter may not matter very much on the battlefield but most military vehicles spend much of their service lives operating alongside civilian traffic so must be correspondingly environmentally-friendly. Further engine efficiency can be expected with the increasing employment of electronic controls for engine monitoring and control and such mundane areas as transmission control. The use of electronics will also spread to braking systems, load management and extend to journey management and navigation.

The introduction of synthetic materials will also make trucks lighter but stronger where it matters, enabling higher potential payloads to be carried.

The greater use of central tyre inflation systems will improve the ability of trucks that normally travel on roads to tackle rough terrain for extended periods. Electrical systems will become more 'solid state' with fewer wiring looms to be damaged or otherwise break while better organised monitoring systems will do away with circuit breakers and fuses.

As far as drivers are concerned the greatest improvements will come about with the so-called ergonomics which will make future military vehicles easier to drive and generally operate by improving small matters such as cab layout and comfort. The increased use of load handling cranes or other material handling devices will enable an individual to perform the load-handling tasks that once required many - this is already happening in many areas as manpower restrictions are inflicted on many armed forces.

One aspect of military vehicles that will not happen is the often forecast prospect for large fleets of ultra-high mobility vehicles. Although the notion of logistics vehicles being able to cross all manner of obstacles may be attractive the fact is that such vehicles would be wildly expensive to the extent that they would be hopelessly uneconomic. Today's military trucks are somehow managing to combine road transport utility with a high degree of cross-country performance, thereby striking a compromise that suits most users. If that compromise somehow becomes unbalanced, as it would were high mobility to be the only objective, things would soon reach the point where costs alone would soon impose their disciplines - unless the vehicle is for some special application. This alone is one reason why most military vehicles continue to run on wheels rather than on tracks.

Things to come - an Oshkosh M1074 palletized Load System 10 x 10 truck carrying 16 tonnes of supplies on a flattrack and towing a trailer carrying a further 16 tonnes, both being loaded and unloaded by the integral PLS load handling system.

Designed to keep running for many years to come, an Oshkosh M911 Heavy Equipment Transporter (HET) towing a semi-trailer carrying a M1 Abrams MBT.

Contents

ENGESA EE - 12 Brazil

The **EE-12** was developed by ENGESA Engenheiros Especializados SA of Sao Paulo during the mid-1980s and is claimed to have an excellent cross country performance. The vehicle is normally driven with an open top with only the forward-folding windscreen for cover. A canvas hood can be erected over a folding frame to provide weather protection for the driver and three passengers; the two removable side doors are canvas.

Originally developed for an overseas customer, the **EE-12** has a strong steel chassis frame with integral front and rear bumpers fitted with towing and lashing shackles; a towing pintle for light trailers or light weapons such as mortars is provided at the rear. If required the rear bench seat can be removed to provide extra cargo stowage space. Standard equipment carried includes a spare wheel at the rear and one jerrican rack.

Weapons such as machine guns can be mounted and a there.is a special anti-tank version with a rearranged layout plus a split windscreen to accommodate a 106 mm recoilless rifle. Other variants include an anti-tank missile carrier, a communications vehicle, and a front line ambulance carrying a single stretcher. It is available powered by either a General Motors 151 2.5 litre petrol engine or a Perkins 3.9 litre diesel.

The **EE-12** has been exported in quantity to Angola (their versions feature a hard-topped body) and to an undisclosed Middle East nation; as far as is known it is not used by the Brazilian armed forces.

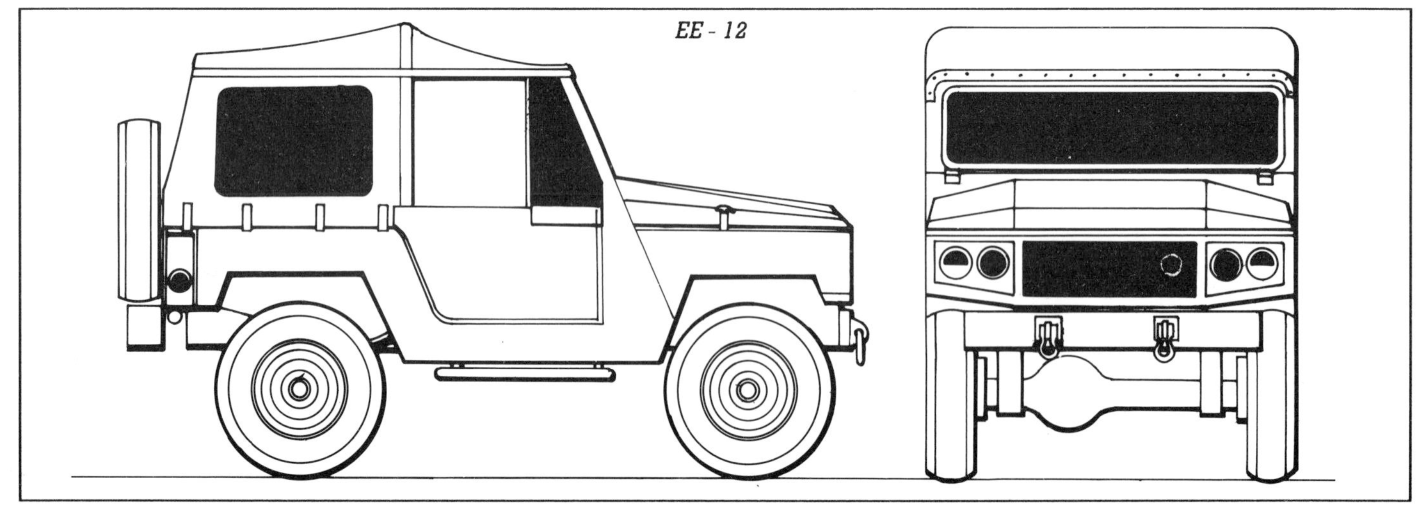
EE - 12

Specification

Role: light utility vehicle and weapons carrier
Cab seating: 1 + 3
Configuration: 4 x 4
Weight: (empty) 1730 kg
Max load: 500 kg
Length: 3.83 m
Width: 1.9 m
Height overall: 1.85 m
Ground clearance: 0.23 m
Track: 1.454 m
Wheelbase: 2.26 m
Max speed: (road) 120 km/h
Fuel capacity: 90 litres
Fording: 0.6 m
Engine: GM 151 2.47 litre petrol or
Perkins 4.2064.236 3.86 litre diesel
Power output: (petrol) 85 hp/4400 rpm
(diesel) 90 hp/3000 rpm
Gearbox: manual 5f, 1r
Clutch: single dry plate
Transfer box: single-speed
Steering: worm and roller
Turning circle: 13.2 m
Suspension: coil spring and shock absorbers
on all wheels
Tyres: 7.50 x 16
Electrical system: 24 V

Variants: see text

ENGESA EE-12 4 x 4 light vehicle with soft top

Volkswagen/Bombardier Iltis Germany/Canada

The first **Volkswagen 183 Iltis** (Polecat) was produced in 1977 in response to a (former) West German Army requirement and by late 1981 8,800 had been produced at Volkswagen's Ingolstadt plant. In 1983 production and worldwide marketing rights (including for civilian sales) were transferred to Bombardier of Canada where production of a further 2,500 units (known as the **Model 183YX**) commenced for the Canadian Armed Forces. Further orders were received from Belgium (2,637 units), Oman and the Cameroons.

The Iltis was designed using the lighter **Auto Union Munga** as a basis and made use of Volkswagen Polo and Audi Quattro commercial components. The body is all steel and there is an integral safety roll bar. The main recognition feature is the long sloping hood and the normal cab cover is a canvas tilt which can be removed for bulky loads.

Various weapons may be carried on optional mounting kits and there is a front line ambulance version. Other versions include a telephone cable layer, a command and/or communication vehicle and a variant carrying sound ranging equipment.

The Iltis can be lifted by a UH-60A Black Hawk helicopter and has been tested for para-dropping. Normally powered by a Volkswagen petrol engine, the Iltis can be supplied with a turbocharged diesel. Other options include a hard top, a winch and a towing hook for unbraked trailers weighing up to 750 kg. Anti-tank missile racks can be fitted.

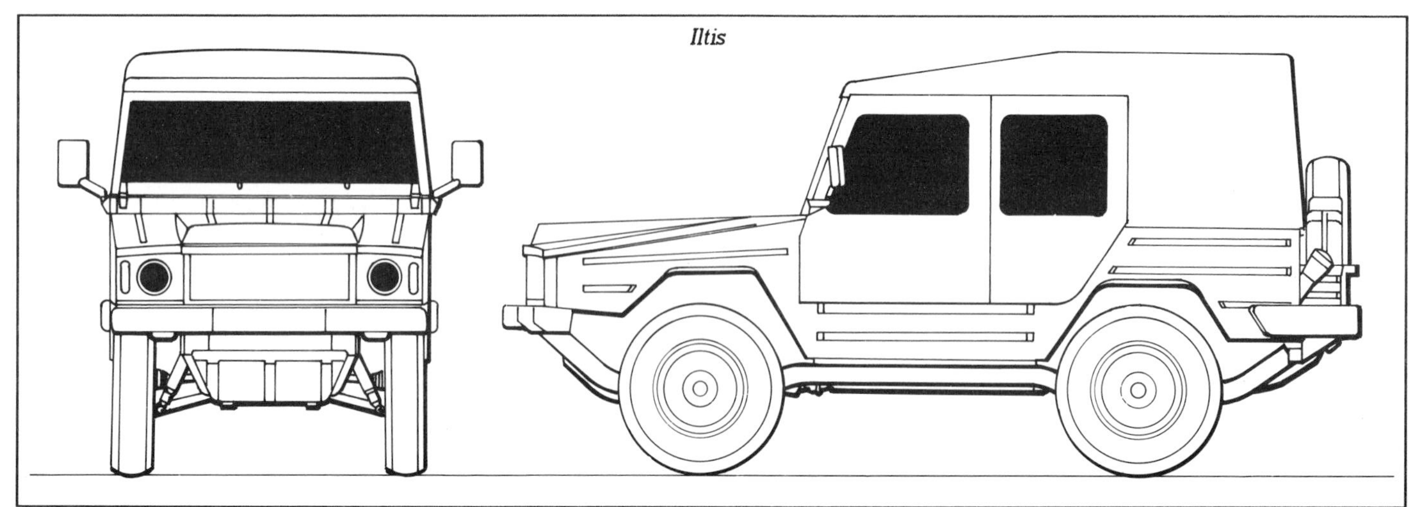
Iltis

Specification

Role: light utility vehicle
Cab seating: 1 + 3
Configuration: 4 x 4
Weight: (empty) 1550 kg
Max load: 500 kg
Length: 3.954 m
Width: 1.52 m
Height: 1.837 m
Ground clearance: 0.225 m
Track: 1.23/1.26 m
Wheelbase: 2.017 m
Max speed: (road) 130 km/h
Fuel capacity: 85 litres
Fording: 0.6 m
Engine: VW 049 1.7 litre petrol
Power output: 74 hp/5000 rpm
Gearbox: VW 005 manual 5f (4f plus crawler), 1 r
Clutch: single dry plate
Transfer box: 2-speed
Steering: rack and pinion
Turning circle: 11 m
Suspension: multi-leaf springs and shock absorbers
Tyres: 6.50 R 16
Electrical system: 24 V

Variants: see text

Bombardier-produced Iltis general purpose vehicle

LOHR Fardier FL 500 and FL 501 France

The **LOHR FL 500** was developed by a company known as SOFRAMAG for French Army airborne units. About 300 were originally produced and are still employed as light load platforms to support airborne forces immediately following an airborne operation.

The vehicle is little more than a flat platform with a seat for the driver, although more troops can be carried on the empty load area.

The driver is provided with an anti-roll safety bar and the entire chassis is tubular steel; the bodywork is mainly aluminium and polyester.

The FL 500 can be para-dropped or carried by a helicopter; two can be carried slung under a SA-330 Puma. A transport aircraft such as a C-130 can carry six vehicles ready for immediate use or 12 as cargo. Once on the ground the **FL 500** can carry up to 500 kg of supplies such as ammunition and can tow a further 500 kg on a light trailer.

The latest version is the **FL 501** with a more powerful air- cooled engine. The overall dimensions remain the same, as does the load carrying performance but the extra power allows loads weighing up to 600 kg to be towed, enabling the **FL 501** to tow weapons such as a Thomson-Brandt 120 mm mortar or a 20 mm anti- aircraft gun.

The **FL 501** has also been trialled as a launch platform for light surface-to-air missiles and as a mobile fire post for anti-tank missiles. Numbers of **FL 500** and **FL 501s** were sold to Argentina and some other countries. In time these vehicles will be replaced by a new lightweight carrier known as the LOHR **VLA**.

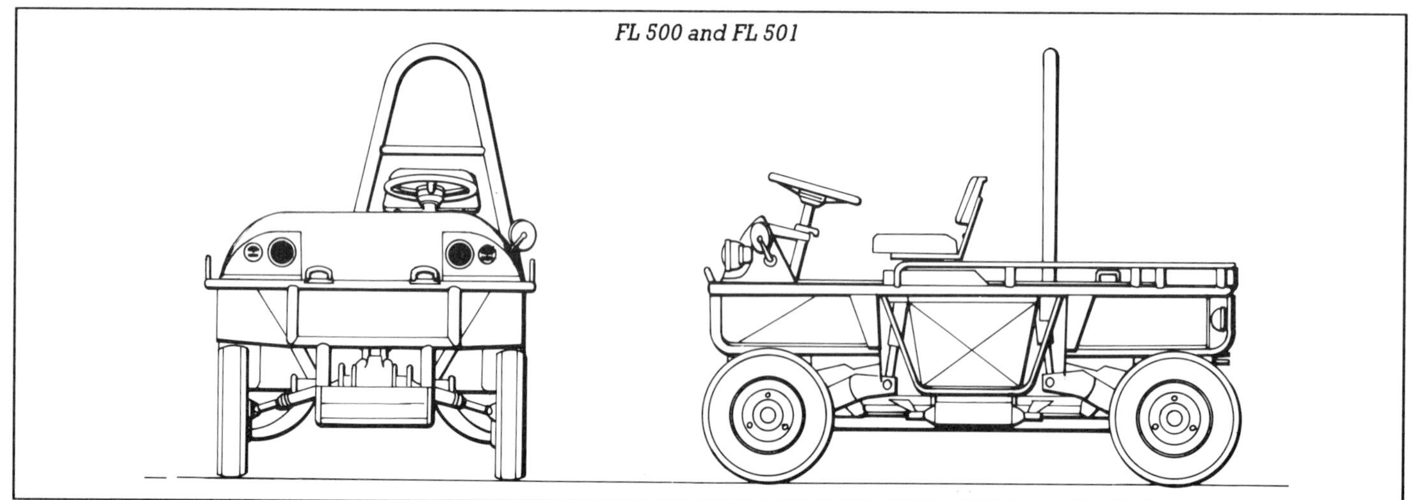

FL 500 and FL 501

Specification

Role: light airportable load carrier
Seating: 1
Configuration: 4 x 4
Weight: (empty) 680 kg
Max load: 500 kg
Length: 2.41 m
Width: 1.5 m
Height: 1.18 m
Ground clearance: (loaded) 0.2 m
Track: 1.26 m
Wheelbase: 1.735 m
Max speed: (road) 80 km/h
Fuel capacity: 25 litres
Fording: 0.4 m
Engine: (FL 500) Citroën 0.6 litre AK 2 flat twin petrol
(FL 501) Citroën V06/630 flat twin petrol
Power output: (FL 500) 29 hp/6750 rpm
(FL 501) 36 hp/5500 rpm
Gearbox: Citroën manual, 4f, 1r
Clutch: single dry plate
Transfer box: 2-speed
Steering: rack and pinion
Turning circle: 9.6 m
Suspension: independent, coil spring and shock absorber
Tyres: 16.5 x 15 M + S
Electrical system: 12 V

Variants: FL 500, FL 501

Lohr FL 501 light vehicle with 120 mm mortar in tow

The Auverland Series

France

Auverland SA of Saint-Germain-Laval took over the assets of the old SAMO concern during the mid-1980s and carried out a revision of the basic SAMO 4 x 4 design which had been extensively exported and which is still produced in Portugal by UMM.

The redesign resulted in a new series of vehicles which now includes the **Type A3** (payload 500 kg), and the larger **Type A2** and **Type SC2**, both powered by a Peugeot XD3P 2.5 litre diesel and with payload capacities of up to 1000 -1100 kg. All these types have a common visual resemblance and are all produced in a variety of wheelbase and chassis lengths to meet specific customer requirements, eg the Type A2 can have a wheelbase length of either 2.35 or 2.75 m. These variations also result in varying payloads for the Types A2 and SC2 and can be increased by the installation of heavy duty suspensions.

Numerous variations can occur in bodywork, ranging from a soft top to station waggon or pick-up versions; if required, vehicles are delivered in bare chassis form. Extras such as winches can be provided and it is possible to fit various types and capacities of petrol engine if required.

All models can accommodate a suppressed 24-volt electrical system for command and communication variants.

All versions are in production and some Type A3s are in use by the French Navy and Air Force.

Most production is for export to North Africa and elsewhere.

The Auverland Series

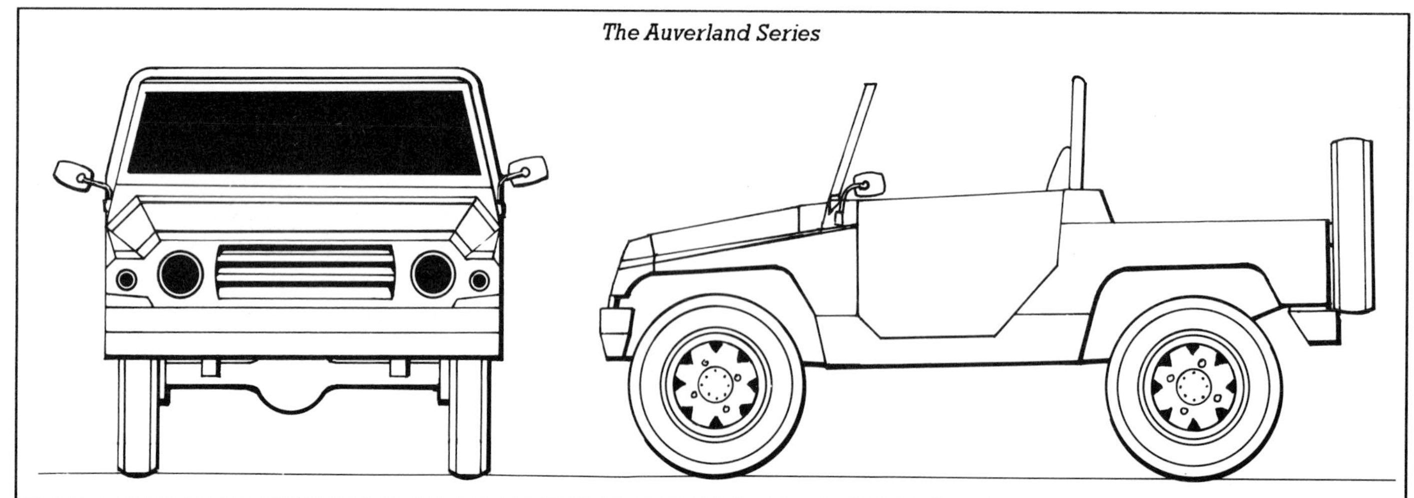

Specification
(Type A3)

Role: light utility vehicle
Cab seating: 1 + up to 5
Configuration: 4 x 4
Weight: (empty) 1150 kg
Max load: 500 kg
Length: 3.65 or 3.85 m
Width: 1.54 m
Height: 1.7 m
Ground clearance: 0.25m
Track: 1.342 m
Wheelbase: 2.25 m
Max speed: (road) 115 km/h
Fuel capacity: 80 litres
Fording: 0.4 m
Engine: Peugeot XUD9 1.9 litre diesel
Power output: 64 hp/4600 rpm
Gearbox: Peugeot BA 7/4 manual, 4f, 1r
Clutch: single dry plate
Transfer box: Auverland A80 2-speed
Steering: mechanical
Turning circle: 10 m
Suspension: coil springs and shock absorbers
Tyres: 6.50 x 16
Electrical system: 12 V

Variants: Type A2, Type A3,
Type SC2

Auverland Type A3 4 x 4 light vehicle

Peugeot P4/Mercedes-Benz 240 GD France/Germany/Greece

The **Mercedes-Benz 240 GD**, and its longer wheelbase version (2.85 m) the **300 GD**, are among the most successful of modern European military vehicles. Over 12,000 were produced for the German armed forces and thousands more have been exported to countries such as Argentina, Switzerland and Norway (and many others). The type is licence-produced in France as the **Peugeot P4** with over 15,000 ordered for the French armed forces. The type is also licence-produced in Greece (5,000 units). Mercedes-Benz production is actually carried out in Austria by GFG of Graz.

The basic model is the **240 GD** powered by a 2.4 litre engine and with a 2.4 m wheelbase. The **300 GD** has a 3 litre diesel and a 2.85 m wheelbase. A 2.3 litre petrol engine is available to power the **230 GD**. Numerous body forms and seating arrangements are possible with the 300 GD capable of seating up to seven plus the driver. Soft and hard-tops are available, including station wagons and vans. An ambulance version is available and there are also cable-laying and NBC decontamination models.

Peugeot produce their own variations including a lightly-armoured personnel or electronic equipment carrier and an air defence version for Mygale missiles; light radar-carrying models have been produced. With the French Army the P4 is known as the *Vehicule de Liason Tout Terrain (VLTT)*. Some French Army P4s are used as mobile MILAN anti- tank missile fire posts. Production continues for both the military and civilian markets.

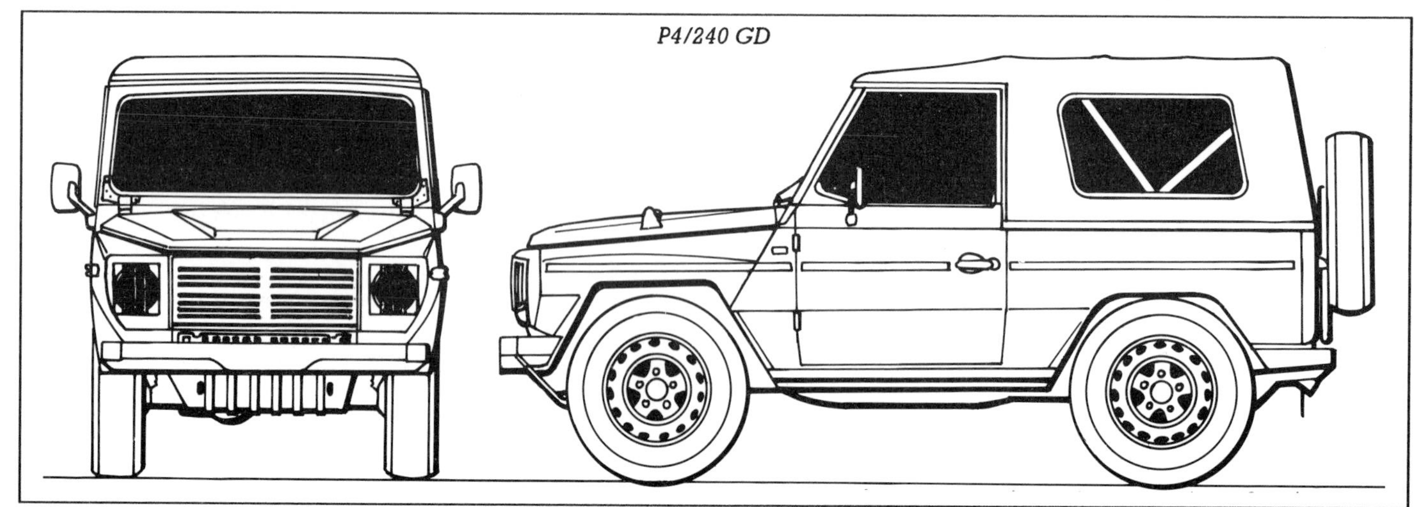
P4/240 GD

Specification

Role: light utility vehicle
Cab seating: 1 + up to 7
Configuration: 4 x 4
Weight: (empty) 1670 kg
Max load: 750 kg
Length: 4.145 m
Width: 1.7 m
Height: 1.995 m
Ground clearance: 0.24 m
Track: 1.425 m
Wheelbase: 2.4 or 2.85 m
Max speed: (road) 117 km/h
Fuel capacity: 70 litres
Fording: 0.6 m
Engine: OM 616 2.4 litre, or OM 617 3 litre, or M115 2.3 litre petrol
Power output: 72 hp/4400 rpm, 88 hp/4400 rpm, 90 hp/5000 rpm
Gearbox: manual, 4f. 1 r
Clutch: single dry plate
Transfer box: VG 080 2-speed
Steering: recirculating ball, power assisted
Turning circle: 11.4 m
Suspension: coil springs and shock absorbers
Tyres: 20.5 R 16
Electrical system: 24 V

Variants: Mercedes-Benz 240 GD, Mercedes-Benz 300 GD, Peugeot P4

Peugeot P4 4 x 4 light vehicle armed with 7.62 mm machine gun

M-242 MMV

For many years the Israeli Defence Forces used M151 and similar Jeep-type vehicles as their standard patrol and reconnaissance vehicles. Experience showed that small Jeep-type models were not ideally suited to military conditions within Israel (although many are still in service) so Automotive Industries Limited of Nazareth Illit developed their **M-242 MMV** (Multi Mission Vehicle). The first prototypes were ready during 1987-88.

The M-242 MMV looks similar to but differs from M151-type vehicles by being larger overall, having a much stronger body and frame, and using a more powerful engine; there are many other detail design differences. The front axle is fully floating while the rear axle is semi-floating.

Produced with one of two frame lengths (4.15 or 4.5 m), the M-242 MMV is intended for front line combat duties as well as routine patrol and utility use. It can therefore be armed with one or more 7.62 mm machine guns while a special anti-tank version carries a 106 mm recoilless rifle at the rear; these armed vehicles are rarely fitted with windscreens or covers. Other combat equipment includes adjustable spotlights and a roll bar behind the driver's position.

Command and general utility versions may have forward-folding windscreens and a soft top. Command versions may have a 24-volt electrical system for their radio equipment. Other optional equipment includes black-out driving lights, a winch, and provision to carry a container carrying electronic or other equipment. It is possible to tow light trailers or weapons such as mortars.

M-242 MMV

Specification

Role: light utility vehicle
Cab seating: 1 + 3 to 5
Configuration: 4 x 4
Weight: (empty) 1800 kg
Max load: 540 kg
Length: 4.15 or 4.5 m
Width: 1.62 m
Height: 1.8 m
Ground clearance: approx 0.25 m
Track: n/av
Wheelbase: n/av
Max speed: (road) 144 km/h
Fuel capacity: 56.7 litres
Fording: approx 0.4 m
Engine: AMC 4.2 litre 6-cylinder diesel
Power output: 115 hp
Gearbox: Tremec T-176, 4f, 1r
Clutch: single dry plate
Transfer box: Dana 300 2-speed
Steering: recirculating ball
Turning circle: 11.46 m
Suspension: leaf springs and shock absorbers
Tyres: 7.00 x 15 8 ply
Electrical system: 12 or 24 V

Variants: see text

An array of M242 MMV (multi-mission vehicles)

FIAT Campagnola 1107 AD

Italy

The **FIAT Campagnola 1107 AD** was placed in production during 1974 to replace the old **FIAT AR-59** (also known as the Campagnola), numbers of which remain in use. Two body lengths were produced, 3.775 and 4.025 m, but both versions had the same wheelbase (2.3 m). Extra seating for up to six passengers on bench seats carried in the rear area, can be fitted into the longer version; the short version accommodates four passengers in the rear. The standard engine was a FIAT 2 litre petrol and at one point a 72 hp diesel unit was offered as an option. A lower compression petrol engine was available along with other special equipment for operations in hot and dusty conditions.

Other options included power-assisted steering and different tyre sizes. Both hard and canvas-topped versions were produced, both with tailgates. The Campagnola was used as the basis for many special conversions such as a light armoured personnel carrier (the **ASA Guardian**) and numerous special bodies, including security vehicles and ambulances manufactured by specialist body makers.

The Italian Army uses the Campagnola as a TOW anti-tank missile carrier and the vehicle is used by some artillery units to tow the OTO Melara 105 mm Pack Howitzer. Command and communications versions with extra radio equipment exist. Some are used by Italian police forces for internal security duties. The Campagnola is no longer in production by FIAT (now IVECO Fiat) but it is still used extensively by the Italian armed forces and Tunisia, to whom 400 units were exported.

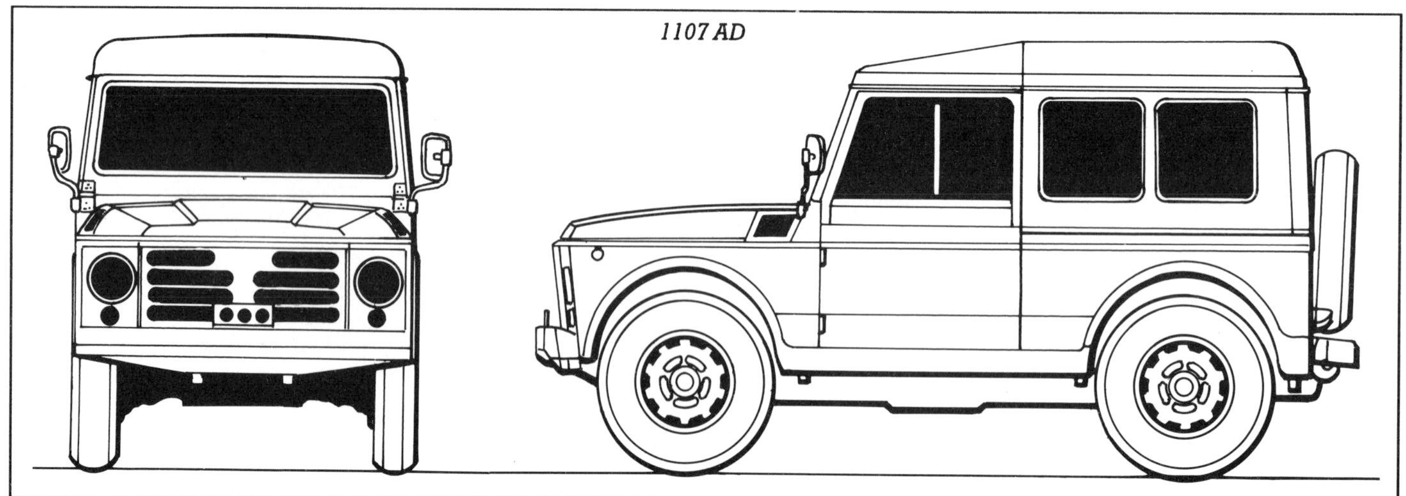
1107 AD

Specification

Role: light utility vehicle
Cab seating: 1 + 5 or 8
Configuration: 4 x 4
Weight: (empty) 1670 or 1740 kg
Max load: 750 kg
Length: 3.775 or 4.025 m
Width: 1.58 m
Height: 1.9 m
Ground clearance: 0.275 m
Track: 1.365 m/1.404 m
Wheelbase: 2.3 m
Max speed: (road) 120 km/h
Fuel capacity: 57 litres
Fording: 0.7 m
Engine: FIAT 2 litre 4-cylinder petrol
Power output: 80 hp/4600 rpm
Gearbox: manual, 5f, 1r
Clutch: single dry plate
Transfer box: 2-speed
Steering: worm and roller
Turning circle: 10.8 m
Suspension: independent strut and link type with torsion bars
Tyres: 7.00 x 16 C
Electrical system: 24 V

Variants: see text

Fiat Campagnola 4 x 4 light vehicle

UMM Alter

Uniaño Metalo-Mecañica Limitada (UMM) of Lisbon developed the **Alter** from the **UMM 490** and **494**, the Portuguese versions of the old French **SAMO** design. With the **Alter**, UMM decided to produce a slightly larger and more powerful vehicle capable of assuming a wide range of roles, including weapon carriers and utility vehicles for civilian organisations. The result is a versatile vehicle that can be produced in several forms. The basic engine is a 2.498 litre 76 hp diesel but also available are a turbocharged version of the same engine developing 115 hp and a 1.971 litre petrol unit developing 108 hp. Short and long wheelbase versions are available with the longer version being able to accommodate the driver, two front passengers and up to ten in the rear on bench seats. The long wheelbase version can carry an on-road payload of up to 1700 kg. The usual array of body types is available.

As a weapons carrier the **Alter** is normally used in a completely open form. As such it can be used to carry a heavy machine gun mounted on a roll bar behind the driver's position, a 106 mm recoilless rifle, or anti-tank missiles such as the SS-11, TOW or MILAN. A special air defence version has racks for Blowpipe missiles and it is possible to tow heavy mortars and other such weapons.

Special police versions are produced and numerous special bodies for use by public utilities are produced, including one model with a hydraulic lift inspection platform. An ambulance with a box body is another variant.

The **Alter** can be para-dropped.

UMM Alter

Specification

Role: light utility vehicle and weapons carrier
Cab seating: 1 + 7 up to 12
Configuration: 4 x 4
Weight: (empty) 1610 or 1770 kg
Max load: (road) 1110 or 1700 kg
Length: 4.17 or 4.857 m
Width: 1.69 m
Height: 1.955 m
Ground clearance: 0.23 m
Track: 1.342 m/1.366 m
Wheelbase: 2.56 or 3.078 m
Max speed: (road) 120 km/h
Fuel capacity: 60 or 90 litres
Fording: 0.6 m
Engine: 2.498 litre 4-cylinder diesel
Power output: 76 hp/4500 rpm
Gearbox: manual, 5f, 1r
Clutch: single dry plate
Transfer box: 2-speed
Steering: worm and roller
Turning circle: 10.5 m
Suspension: leaf springs and shock absorbers
Tyres: 6.50 x 16 or 7.00 x 16
Electrical system: 12 or 24 V

Variants: see text

UMM Alter 4 x 4 light vehicle armed with 12.7 mm heavy machine gun

UAZ-469B

Former Soviet Union

The prototype **UAZ-469** was produced in 1961 but production of the fully developed version, the **UAZ-469B**, did not commence until late 1972 and the first service versions were delivered during 1973. Since then tens of thousands of **UAZ- 469Bs** have been produced at the Ul'yanovsk Motor Vehicle Plant and they have been exported for military and civil use (the civilian version is marketed as the **Tundra**) to wherever Soviet influence spread. The **UAZ-469B** (latest designation **UAZ-31512**) is a conventional design powered by the engine of the **Volga GAZ-21A(E)** car with seating for the driver, one passenger and a further six passengers in the rear on inward-facing bench seats although alternative seating arrangements are possible. The normal top is a canvas tilt over removable bows but a hard top is an option.

Since the **UAZ-469B** has been distributed widely, there are many locally-introduced variations such as the RPG-7 anti-tank rocket launcher version introduced by Iraq, and numerous types of mobile radio communication centres are in Warsaw Pact and other service. Van-bodied versions have been produced and one specially-equipped version, the **UAZ-469-RKh**, is used by the Russian Army as an NBC reconnaissance vehicle which is used to emplace lane markers along paths cleared through contaminated areas. The **UAZ-3152** (or **UAZ- 469BG**) is a front line ambulance. The latest production version is the **UAZ-3151** which uses coil springs for the front suspension and a more powerful (83 hp) engine. Some bodywork modifications have also been introduced.

The design of the Chinese **BJ-212** was influenced by the **UAZ-469B.**

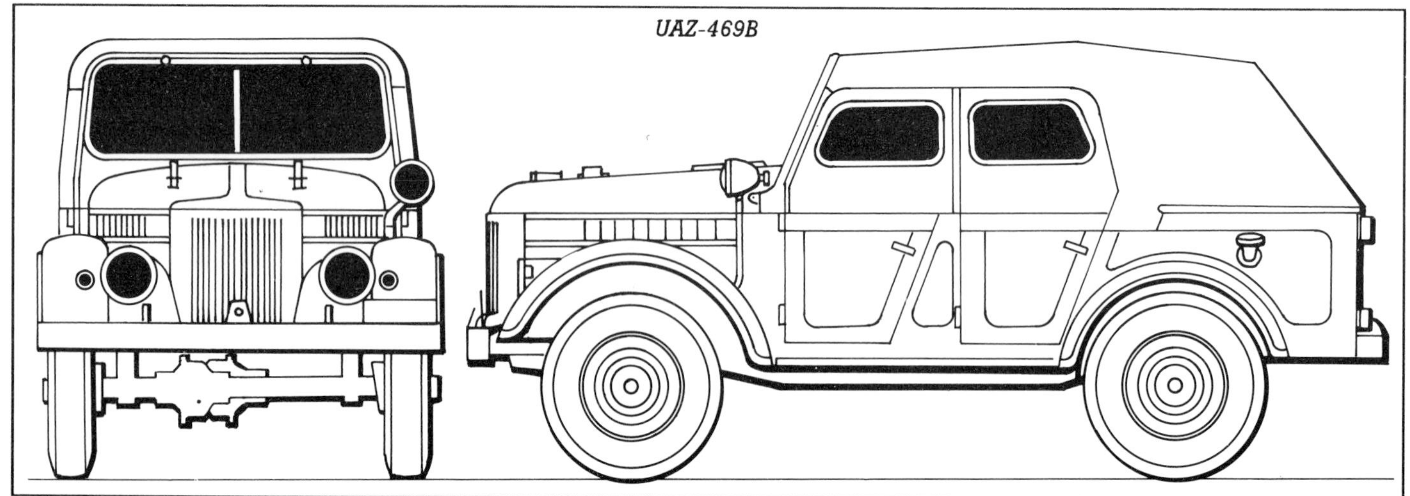

UAZ-469B

Specification

Role: light utility vehicle
Cab seating: 1 + 6
Configuration: 4 x 4
Weight: (empty) 1540 kg
Max load: 600 kg
Length: 4.025 m
Width: 1.785 m
Height: 2.015 m
Ground clearance: 0.22 m
Track: 1.422 m
Wheelbase: 2.38 m
Max speed: (road) 100 km/h
Fuel capacity: 78 litres
Fording: 0.7 m
Engine: ZMZ-451M 2.445 litre 4-cylinder petrol
Power output: 75 hp/4000 rpm
Gearbox: manual, 4f, 1r
Clutch: single dry plate
Transfer box: 2-speed
Steering: mechanical
Turning circle: 13 m
Suspension: leaf springs and shock absorbers
Tyres: 8.40 x 15
Electrical system: 12 V

Variants: UAZ-469, UAZ-469B, UAZ-469BG, UAZ-469R, UAZ-RKh, UAZ- 3151, UAZ-31512, UAZ-3152

UAZ-469 4 x 4 light vehicle

The Land Rovers

The **Land Rover** has been one of the UK's most successful automobile designs ever since the first example was produced in 1948. Over the years many models and variations have been introduced culminating in the **Land Rover One Ten** of 1983. The One Ten introduced the coil spring suspension of the **Range Rover**, a longer wheelbase, revised bodywork and detail design changes. Three engines are available, a 3.5 litre V-8 petrol and two 2.5 litre engines, one petrol and one diesel (with optional turbocharging). Optional features include power steering and numerous types of body. The One Ten was followed by the **Land Rover Ninety** with a shorter (2.36 m) wheelbase and later by the larger capacity **Land Rover 127** (wheelbase 3.226 m). All these Land Rovers are used as the basis for many specialised vehicles from light fire tenders to ambulances and weapon carriers.

Armoured and mine-protected versions have been produced. 6 x 6 conversions of the **One Ten** have been developed, including an Australian model by **JRA** (qv). The **4 x 4 One Ten** is also produced in Australia, powered by a Japanese Isuzu 3.9 litre diesel for the Australian Army.

Elsewhere, Land Rovers are used as air defence and anti-tank missile launch vehicles, as artillery rocket launchers, as combat engineer vehicles carrying digging equipment, and as mobile workshops. Their versatility seems unbounded and numerous variants will continue to appear. Production totals are already in the hundreds of thousands and production continues.

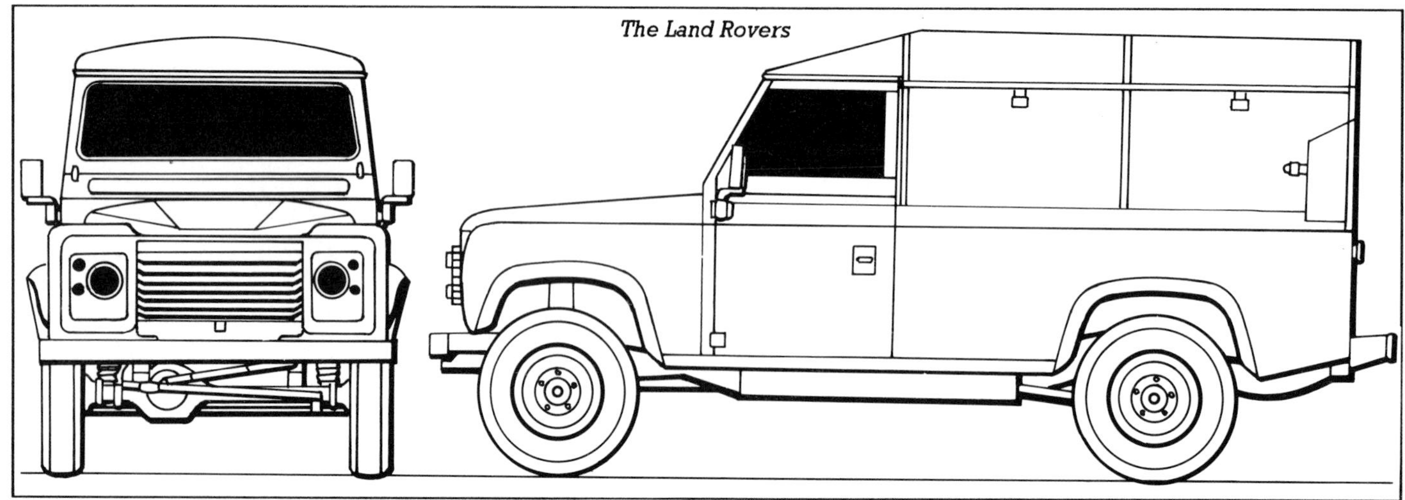
The Land Rovers

Specification

(Land Rover One Ten)

Role: light utility vehicles
Cab seating: 1 + 2 (up to 10 in rear)
Configuration: 4 x 4
Weight: (empty) 3050 kg
Max load: 1486 kg
Length: 4.631 m
Width: 1.79 m
Height: 2.035 m
Ground clearance: 0.216 m
Track: 1.486 m
Wheelbase: 2.794 m
Max speed: (road) approx 100 km/h
Fuel capacity: 79.5 litres
Fording: 0.5 m
Engine: LR 2.495 litre 4-cylinder turbocharged diesel
Power output: 85 hp/4000 rpm
Gearbox: manual, 5f, 1r
Clutch: diaphragm spring
Transfer box: LT230T 2-speed
Steering: recirculating ball (power assistance optional)
Turning circle: 12.8 m
Suspension: coil spring and telescopic dampers
Tyres: 7.50 x 16
Electrical system: 12 or 24 V

Variants: Land Rover Ninety, One Ten, 127

Land Rover One Ten 4 x 4 with hard top

M151 Series

USA

During and after WW2 the Jeep was a virtual symbol of American military influence. Jeeps continued to be manufactured after 1945 in bewildering numbers (and still are in many countries). American service Jeeps were developed through the **M38** series until the **M151** appeared in 1952. It was 1960 before the first **M151** production examples were turned out by Ford. Still easily recognisable as a 'Jeep' the **M151** was known as the **'Mutt'** (from Military Utility Tactical Truck). It was replaced in production by the **M151A1**, with an improved suspension system, in 1964 and the **M151A2** followed in 1970 with more suspension changes, a dual brake system and a folding steering column,plus other changes. In late 1986 a retrofit programme to fit anti-roll bars to over 11,000 US armed forces **M151s** was announced. At one time **M151** production totals were reaching 18,000 a year and eventually **M151**-series vehicles were in service in over 100 countries. Derivatives of the basic vehicle were the **M825** carrying a 106 mm recoilless rifle and the **M718** and **M718A1** forward area ambulances.

The basically-similar **M107** and **M108** were radio vehicles. The basic **M151A2** can be adapted to carry either a machine gun or a TOW anti-tank missile launcher and many US **M825s** were modified back to **M151A2** standard using a special kit, once the 106 mm rifles were withdrawn from service. Light trailers weighing up to 680 kg can be towed across country.

The M151 series was gradually phased out of production during the late 1980s as the engines could no longer meet exhaust emission standards. Any remaining US Army examples are being replaced in service by the **HMMWV** (qv).

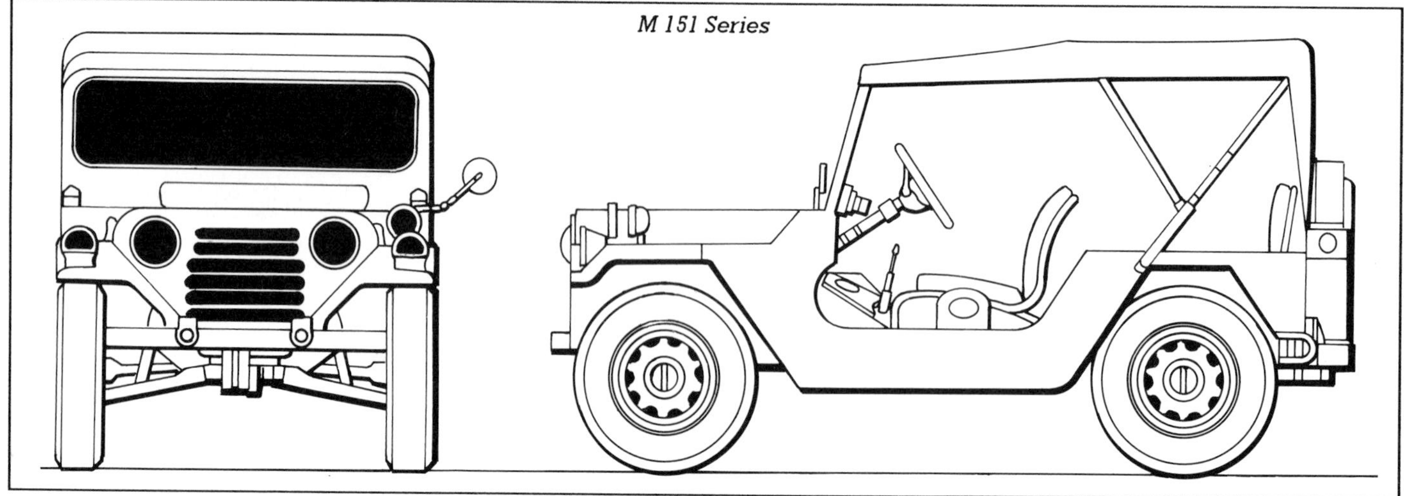

M 151 Series

Specification

(M151A2)

Role: light utility vehicle
Cab seating: 1 + 3
Configuration: 4 x 4
Weight: (empty) 1107 kg
Max load: 363 kg
Length: 3.371 m
Width: 1.633 m
Height: 1.803 m
Ground clearance: 0.24 m
Track: 1.346 m
Wheelbase: 2.159 m
Max speed: (road) 90 km/h
Fuel capacity: 59.8 litres
Fording: 0.53 m
Engine: L-142 2.319 litre 4-cylinder petrol
Power output: 72 hp/4000 rpm
Gearbox: manual, 4f, 1r
Clutch: single dry plate
Transfer box: single-speed
Steering: worm and double roller
Turning circle: 11.27 m
Suspension: coil springs and shock absorbers
Tyres: 7.00 x 16
Electrical system: 24 V

Variants: M151, M151A1, M151A2, M197, M108, M718, M718A1, M825

US Army M151 4 x 4 in typical military setting

IMV 0.75 - 4 x 4 Yugoslavia (Serbia and Montenegro)

The Red Flag Factory in Kragujevac, Serbia, produced the Italian **FIAT AR-59 Campagnola** under licence for many years as the **Zastava AR-51**.

During the mid-1980s Yugoslav vehicle designers used their AR-51 experience to develop a larger vehicle which emerged as the **IMV 0.75 - 4 x 4**. In some ways the **IMV 0.75** visually resembles the later **FIAT Campagnola 1107 AD** (qv) but the overall dimensions are larger all round and the payload is increased to seven passengers (plus the driver) or 750 kg of payload.

The body has a semi-forward control cab and is manufactured mainly using flat pressed steel sheets welded together on a strong welded steel chassis.

Only one style of weather cover is normally offered, a canvas tilt over removable bows. To reduce height even further for air or other transport once the tilt has been removed, the windscreen can be folded forward; the overall height is then only 1.45 m.

Water obstacles up to 0.9 m deep can be crossed following preparation using a special kit. Production and spares holdings are assisted by the front and rear axles being identical. It is anticipated that the **IMV 0.75** will assume many of the Yugoslav armed forces roles formerly carried out by the AR-51. These include towing light artillery pieces, such as the 76 mm M48 mountain gun, and 120 mm mortars.

The current status of this vehicle is uncertain due to the recent disturbances in the region.

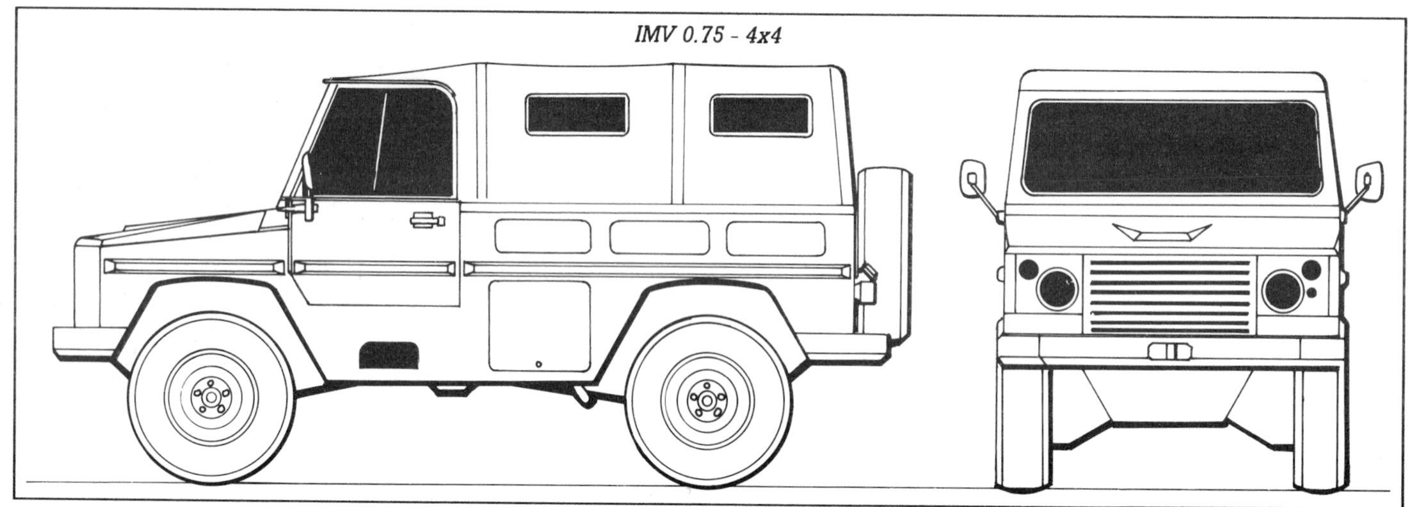
IMV 0.75 - 4x4

Specification

Role: light utility vehicle
Cab seating: 1 + 7
Configuration: 4 x 4
Weight: (empty) 2180 kg
Max load: 750 kg
Length: 4.2 m
Width: 1.74 m
Height: 2.1 m
Ground clearance: 0.29 m
Track: 1.456 m
Wheelbase: 2.5 m
Max speed: (road) 120 km/h
Fuel capacity: n/av
Fording: 0.7 m (0.9 m with preparation)
Engine: S54V 2.45 litre 4-cylinder diesel
Power output: 74 hp/4200 rpm
Gearbox: manual, 5f, 1r
Clutch: single dry plate
Transfer box: 2-speed
Steering: rack and pinion
Turning circle: 11 m
Suspension: independent coil springs with shock absorbers
Tyres: 24.5 x 16
Electrical system: 24 V

Variants: see text

Serbian IMV 0.75 - 4 x 4 light vehicle

JRA Land Rover 110 Heavy Duty 6 x 6 — Australia

Development of the JRA (Jaguar Rover Australia) began in 1981 and following an Australian Army selection programme known as Project Perentie, 400 6 x 6 versions of the Land Rover One Ten were ordered. Fitted with 3.9 litre Isuzu diesels and known as the **JRA Land Rover 110 Heavy Duty 6 x 6**, the first production examples were handed over in March 1989; production of the Army order will continue until 1991. The 110 Heavy Duty is wider than the standard One Ten and is produced in several versions. The base model is a 2 tonne cargo vehicle, with or without a winch. Additionally it can carry up to 12 troops on inward-facing seats on a removable cargo/personnel carrier tray with a soft top. Once removed the tray can be replaced by various workshop modular bodies or bodies configured for carrying Rapier or RBS 70 air defence missile systems. The modular workshop bodies are fitted directly to the chassis frame and can be removed for use on the ground.

There is also an ambulance body and a machine gun- carrying special long range patrol version for the Australian Army's SAS Regiment. Other variants available include a fire truck and a shelter transporter. An enlarged crew cab is also available.

In all these versions the 110 Heavy Duty has a good cross country performance and is well able to absorb the rough knocks of the Australian terrain.

The vehicle has been offered for export and a version with a GM 6.2 litre diesel engine and cold weather equipment was proposed for a possible Canadian Armed Forces application.

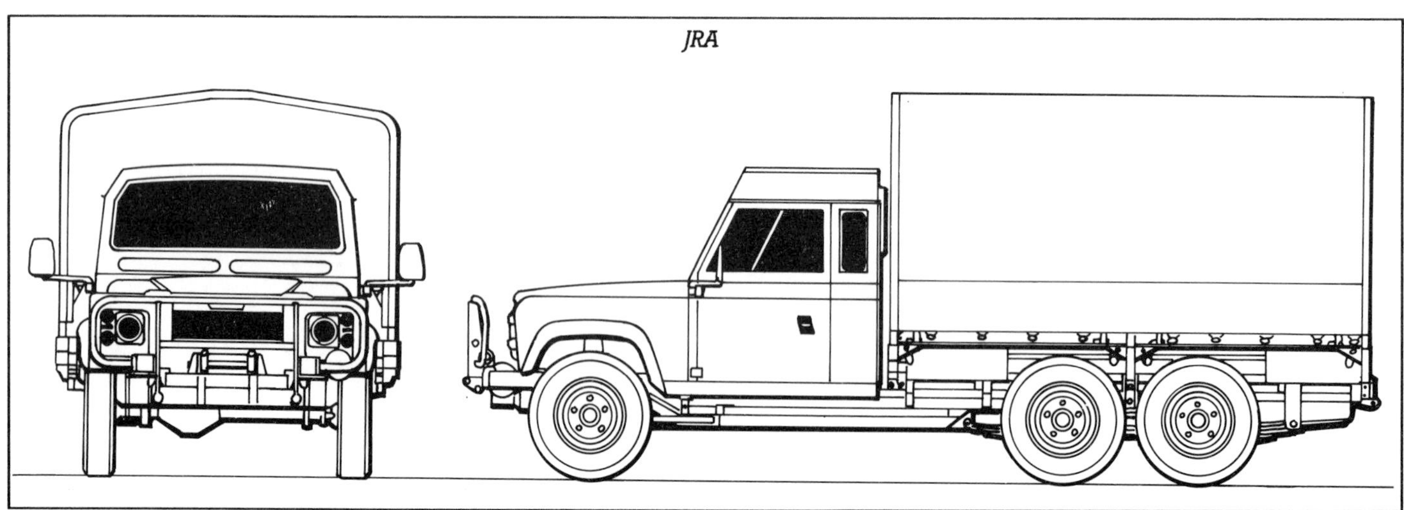

Specification

Role: light truck
Cab seating: 1 + 1 (up to 12 in rear)
Configuration: 6 x 6
Weight: (empty) 3600 kg
Max load: 2000 kg
Length: 6 m
Width: 2.2 m
Height: 2.08 m
Ground clearance: 0.215 m
Track: 1.698 m
Wheelbase: 3.04 m + 0.9 m
Max speed: (road) 100 km/h
Fuel capacity: 130 litres
Fording: approx 0.5 m
Engine: Isuzu 4BDT 3.9 litre 4-cylinder turbo-charged diesel
Power output: 121 hp/3000 rpm
Gearbox: LT95A manual, 4f, 1r
Clutch: single dry plate
Transfer box: 2-speed
Steering: worm and peg with power assistance
Turning circle: 17.2 m
Suspension: coil spring front, leaf spring rear
Tyres: 7.50 x 16
Electrical system: 12 or 24 V

Variants: see text

Land Rover 110 Heavy Duty 6 x 6 light truck in personnel carrier configuration

The Pinzgauers

The first 4 x 4 **Pinzgauer**, powered by a 2.5 litre petrol engine, was produced in 1965 and ever since then the Pinzgauer series has been a major Steyr-Daimler-Puch product. The 4 x 4 vehicles were soon joined by a 6 x 6 version and by 1985 over 20,000 had been produced, nearly all for military users. From 1983 onwards the petrol-engined Pinzgauers were joined by turbocharged diesel-engined versions, the so-called **Turbo D** range, which in most respects were overall improvements on the earlier models. They are known as the **716 series** (4 x 4) and **718 series** (6 x 6) and have longer wheelbases, disc brakes and increased fuel capacities. Other features such as automatic level control systems that enable the superstructure to rise or fall to suit the load involved also became available.

In all their forms the Pinzgauers have been produced in a bewildering array of models with hard or soft-tops, equipped for carrying either passengers or cargo. Some versions have provision to carry weapon system or communication shelters. There are also command versions and some examples were used to carry 20 mm anti-aircraft guns. Ambulance versions with special panel bodies have been manufactured.

All Pinzgauers have an excellent cross country performance and are particularly favoured by Austrian Army alpine units.

An experimental petrol-engined 8 x 8 version was produced in prototype form but was not placed in production.

Exports have been made to nations such as Yugoslavia, Oman, Switzerland and Tunisia, as well as nations in South America. A late variant of the Pinzgauer was selected as a light artillery tractor by the British Army.

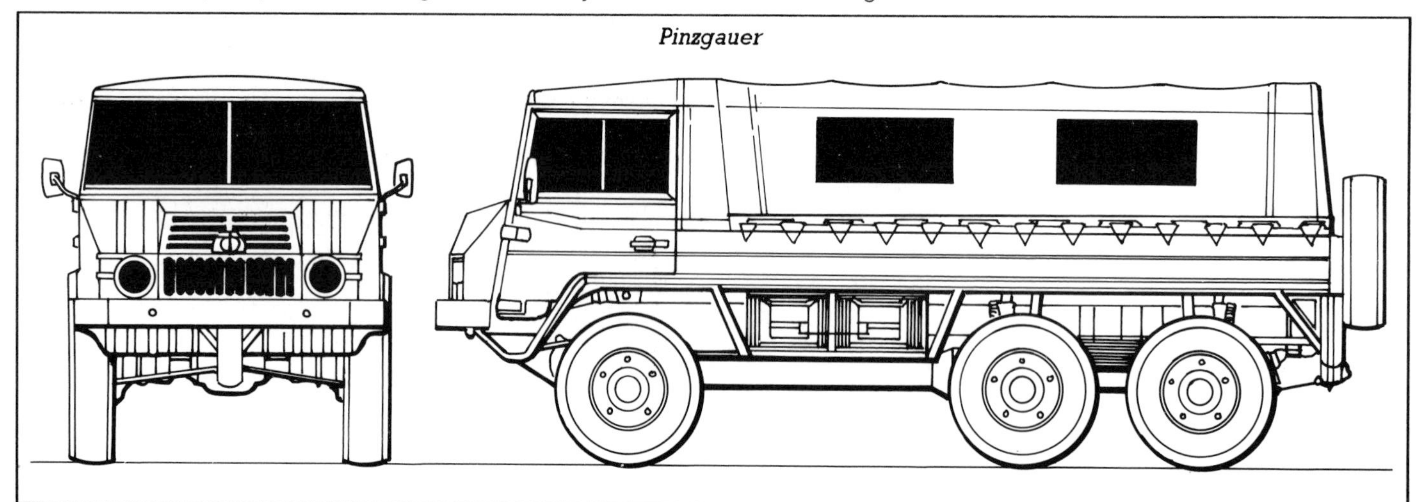

Pinzgauer

Specification

(Pinzgauer 716 M)

Role: all-terrain light utility vehicle
Cab seating: 1 + 9
Configuration: 4 x 4
Weight: (empty) 2200 kg
Max load: 1300 kg
Length: 4.48 m
Width: 1.8 m
Height: 2.045 m
Ground clearance: 0.335 m
Track: 1.52 m
Wheelbase: 2.4 m
Max speed: (road) 122 km/h
Fuel capacity: 145 litres
Fording: 0.7 m
Engine: 2.383 litre 6-cylinder diesel
Power output: 105 hp/4350 rpm
Gearbox: ZF S 5-18/3 manual, 5f, 1r
Clutch: single dry plate
Transfer box: 2-speed
Steering: ZF-Gemmer, power assisted
Turning circle: 11.5 m
Suspension: helical springs
Tyres: 235/85 R 16
Electrical system: 12 or 24 V

Variants: see text

Oman armed forces Pinzgauers carrying communication shelter bodies

Steyr 12 M 18 and 12 M 21 — Austria

Steyr-Daimler-Puch AG describe their **12 M 18** and **12 M 21** trucks as new generation designs for the first of them was produced during 1985 and production commenced in 1986. The two vehicles are essentially similar, the main difference being in the rated output of their otherwise similar turbocharged diesel engines; the 12 M 17 engine develops 177 hp while that for the 12 M 21 develops 210 hp. Both have forward control cabs that can be tilted forward for maintenance and repairs and the cargo bodies are all-steel. The cargo bodies can have folding seats for up to 18 troops seated back-to-back.

To date production has centred on the cargo version which is used by the Austrian Army (well over 2000 units delivered) and by the Canadian Armed Forces in West Germany where they are used by airfield repair units.

The basic design can also be adapted as an artillery tractor, a field ambulance, a recovery vehicle, a fire tender, for carrying shelters and containers, a workshop vehicle and as a tanker.

The Steyr can also be adapted to become a weapon system carrier.

The basic 12 M 18/12 M 21 design is the basis for the US Army's **Family of Medium Tactical Vehicles (FMTV)** selection programme. For this Steyr have teamed with Stewart & Stevenson Services of Houston, Texas. The FMTV programme involves both 4 x 4 and 6 x 6 trucks so the basic 12 M 18 is being developed accordingly.

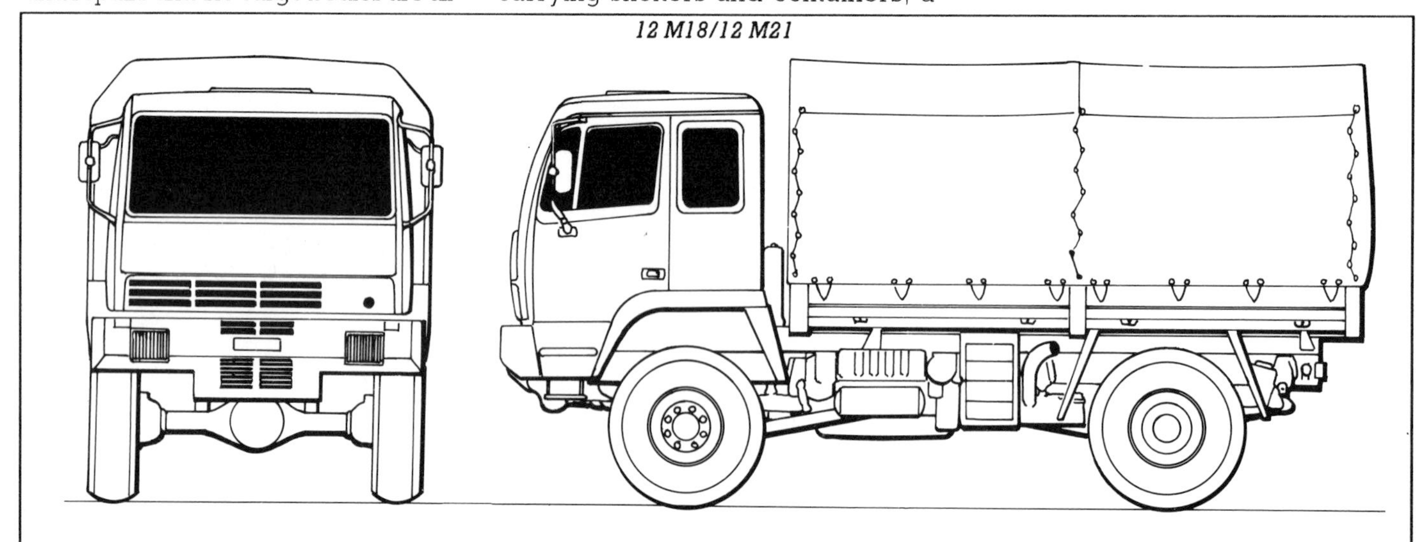
12 M18/12 M21

Specification

Role: general purpose truck
Cab seating: 1 + 1 (up to 18 in rear)
Configuration: 4 x 4
Weight: (empty) 6300 kg
Max load: 5200 kg
Length: 6.36 m
Width: 2.5 m
Height: 3.24 m
Ground clearance: 0.3 m
Track: 2.061 m/2.005 m
Wheelbase: 3.5 m
Max speed: (road) approx 100 km/h
Fuel capacity: 180 litres
Fording: 0.8 m
Engine: Steyr Model WD 612.74 6.6 litre 6-cylinder turbocharged diesel
Power output: (12 M 18) 177 hp/2400 rpm (12 M 21) 210 hp/2400 rpm
Gearbox: ZF 9 S109 manual, 9f, 1r
Clutch: single dry plate
Transfer box: Steyr VG 1200 2-speed
Steering: ZF recirculating ball, power assisted
Turning circle: 14.6 m
Suspension: parabolic leaf springs and shock absorbers
Tyres: 14.5 R 20 MPT
Electrical system: 24

Variants: see text

Austrian Army Steyr 12 M 21 5-tonne truck

Steyr 14 M 14

The **Steyr 14 M 14** is one example of a recent trend in truck design where readily-available components are combined to produce relatively low cost military vehicles for armed forces where more sophisticated products are not required. The **14 M 14** started life as a proposed 4 x 2 truck for sales to Nigeria but it was converted to a 4 x 4 model by adding the transfer case used with the **Steyr 680 M** 4 x 4 truck and the front axle from the **12 M 18/12 M 21** series (see previous entry). Other components come from other Steyr vehicle products. The end result is a thoroughly serviceable utility truck capable of carrying payloads of up to 8000 kg on roads. Up to 18 passengers can be carried on folding bench seats in the cargo area which is normally covered by a canvas tilt.

The **14 M 14** has a forward-control all-steel cab that can be tilted forward for maintenance and the cargo body is also all-steel. Fittings for carrying shelters are provided and the vehicle can also be used to tow artillery pieces or trailers weighing up to 6000 kg.

Optional extras include a 5000 kg rearward operating winch, an electro-hydraulic tailgate lift platform, blackout lighting and a machine gun mounting on the cab roof. Right-hand drive and a driver training version with an enlarged cab are also available.

Sales have been made to Cyprus and to the Canadian Armed Forces operating in Europe. The type is also licence-produced in Greece by ELBO where it is known as the **14ME14/4 x 4**.

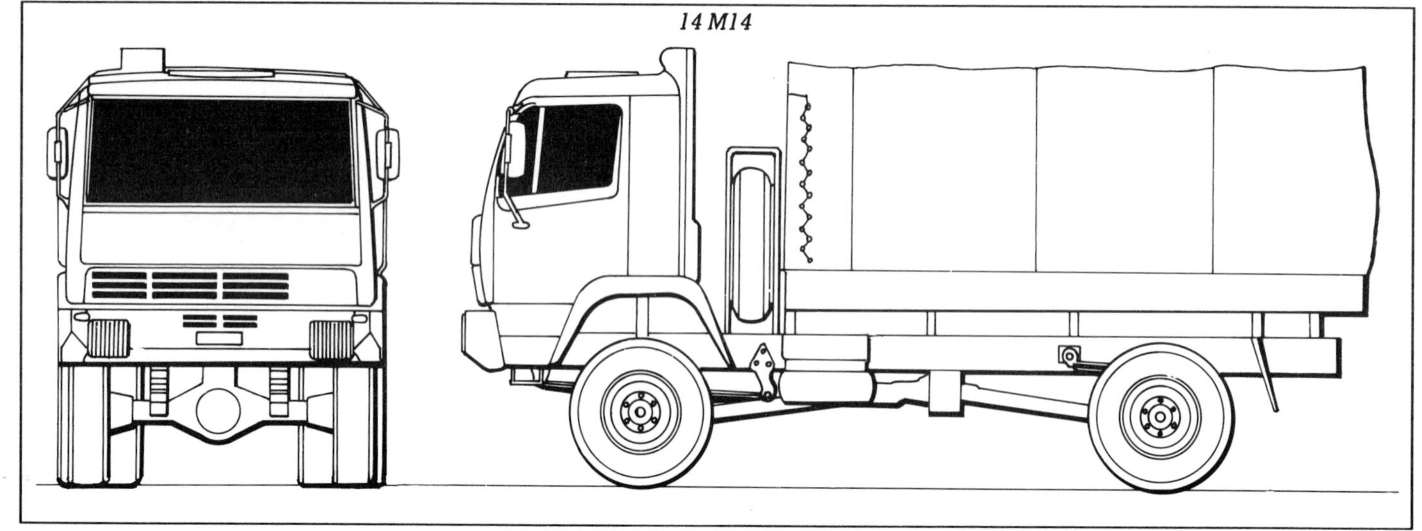
14 M14

Specification

Role: general purpose truck
Cab seating: 1 + 1 (up to 18 in rear)
Configuration: 4 x 4
Weight: (empty) 6000 kg
Max load: up to 8000 kg
Length: 6.62 m
Width: 2.5 m
Height: 3.025 m
Ground clearance: 0.275 m
Track: 1.872 m/1.721 m
Wheelbase: 3.7 m
Max speed: (road) approx 80 km/h
Fuel capacity: 160 litres
Fording: 0.8 m
Engine: Steyr WD 612.22 6.6 litre 6-cylinder diesel
Power output: 136 hp/2400 rpm
Gearbox: Steyr A 51/5 manual, 5f, 1r
Clutch: single dry plate
Transfer box: Steyr VG 450 2-speed
Steering: ZF recirculating ball
Turning circle: 15.2 m leaf springs and shock absorbers
Tyres: 9.00 R 20
Electrical system: 12 or 24 V

Variants: see text

Steyr 14 M 14 8-tonne truck produced for Nigeria

Steyr 1491.330/6 x 6M and Percheron Austria

The first of the **Steyr 1491-series** trucks appeared during the 1980s and it is now one of Steyr's most important and successful products.

There are several vehicles in the range, such as the **Steyr 1491.280/6 x 6M** with a less powerful 9.725 litre engine, but they all follow the same general layout with a forward-control cab and an all-steel cargo body. The Steyr **1491.330/6 x 6M** mentioned in the Specification was designed as an artillery tractor with a gun crew shelter occupying some of the cargo space, while the **1491.6 x 6M** is the general utility truck version. There is also a recovery variant (**1491.260.K34/6 x 6**) and a tank transporter truck tractor (the **1491.330.S34/6 x 6**).

Perhaps the most significant variant is the version produced under licence in Canada by UTDC Inc of Kingston, Ontario. Known as the **Percheron**. 1,200 **Percheron** were manufactured to provide the Canadian Armed Forces with their **Heavy Logistic Vehicle Wheeled (HLVW)**; the name **Percheron** has been applied. There will be several **Percheron** variants including the basic cargo version (with or without a winch, some with a hydraulic crane), a recovery version, a truck tractor, a dumper, a combined floating bridge section or flatrack carrier, and a field repair version known as the **Heavy Mobile Repair Team (HMRT)**; the latter will operate with armoured and artillery units.

The **1491.6 x 6** was selected for licence production in China.

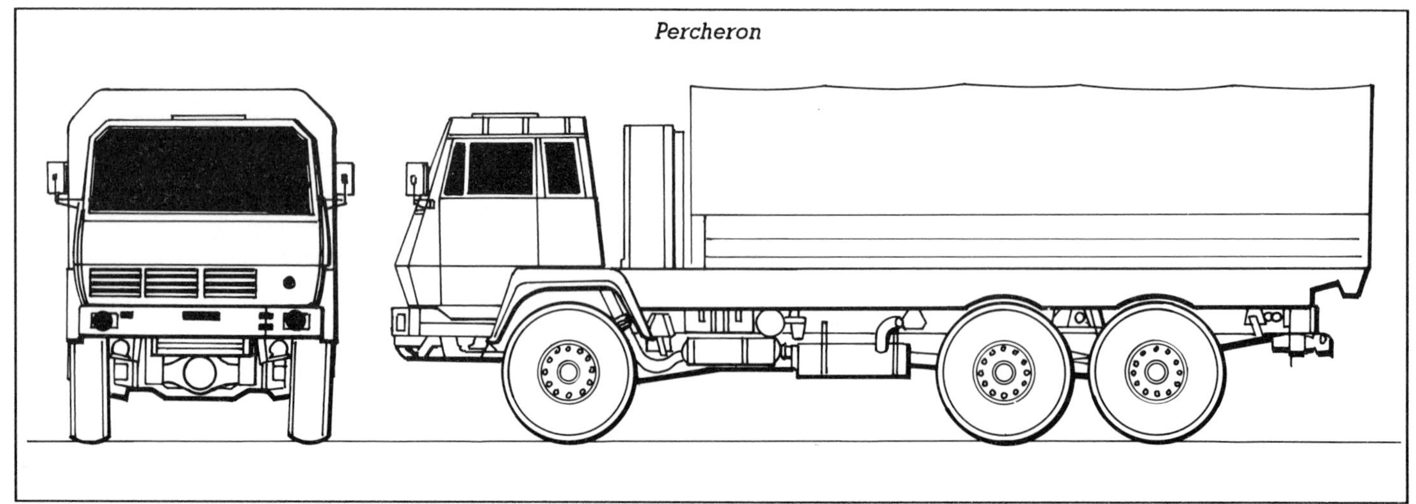

Percheron

Specification

Role: general utility truck and artillery tractor
Cab seating: 1 + 1 or 2
Configuration: 6 x 6
Weight: (empty) 11,800 kg
Max load: 10,700 kg
Length: 8.389 m
Width: 2.5 m
Height: 3.025 m
Ground clearance: 0.37 m
Track: 2.072 m
Wheelbase: 4 m + 1.4 m
Max speed: (road) 85 km/h
Fuel capacity: 400 litres
Fording: 0.8 m
Engine: Steyr WD 815.74 11.97 litre V-8 turbocharged diesel
Power output: 340 hp/2200 rpm
Gearbox: ZF 5 S 111 GP manual, 9f, 1r
Clutch: single dry plate
Transfer box: Steyr VG 1200 2-speed
Steering: ZF 8046 hydraulic
Turning circle: 20.2 m
Suspension: leaf springs and shock absorbers
Tyres: 14.00 R 20
Electrical system: 24 V

Variants: 1491.280/6 x 6, 1491.330/6 x 6M, 1491.6 x 6M, 1491.260.K34/6 x 6, 1491.330.S34/6 x 6, Percheron

Canadian Armed Forces Percheron 10-tonne truck

ENGESA EE-25 Brazil

The **ENGESA EE-25**[series first appeared during the early 1970s and over the years has been powered by a variety of engines; the Mercedes-Benz engine is the latest of a line that includes Chrysler and Perkins units. The series is also unusual in being produced with both 4 x 4 and 6 x 6 drive configurations with the 4 x 4 version being the original version. Both have the same payload characteristics and can carry up to 5,000 kg on roads. Both versions usually have a vinyl-topped cab and a vinyl tilt over bows covering the cargo area.

The **EE-25** has been exported widely outside Brazil, where it is used for commercial as well as military purposes.

Many **EE-25**s have been sold in the Middle East and a significant number were delivered to Angola. The Angolan versions feature a strengthened chassis frame and bodywork changes, plus the addition of an air cleaner to the side of the bonnet.

Libya has been another customer with their examples including a 4 x 4 NBC decontamination variant. Numerous other variants have been produced including an ambulance, crash and fire tenders, a recovery version, fuel and water tankers, mobile workshops and van-bodied models used for command and communications. A shelter-carrying version is also available.

The 6 x 6 versions all feature the ENGESA 'Boomerang' rear axle with its walking beam suspension which enables the **EE-25** to cross very rough terrain while keeping the load platform relatively stable.

The EE-25 is still in production.

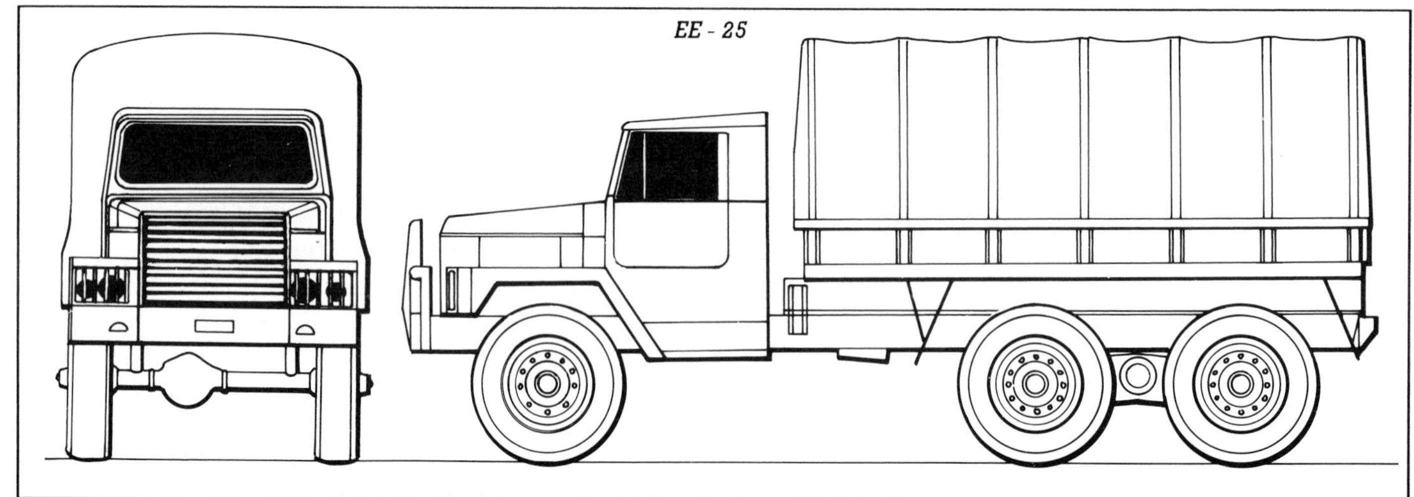

Specification

Role: general utility truck
Cab seating: 1 + 2
Configuration: 6 x 6
Weight: (empty) 7100 kg
Max load: 2500 kg
Length: 6.99 m
Width: 2.25 m
Height: 2.5 m
Ground clearance: 0.27 m
Track: 1.78 m
Wheelbase: 4.2 m
Max speed: (road) 80 km/h
Fuel capacity: 200 litres
Fording: 0.9 m
Engine: MB OM 352A 5.675 litre 6-cylinder diesel
Power output: 156 hp/2800 rpm
Gearbox: manual, 5f, 1r
Clutch: single dry plate
Transfer box: ENGESA 2-speed
Steering: hydraulic
Turning circle: 19 m
Suspension: front, leaf springs and shock absorbers; rear, leaf springs and ENGESA Boomerang rear axle with walking beams
Tyres: 11.00 x 20-14 PR
Electrical system: 24 V

Variants: see text

ENGESA EE-25 6 X 6 truck as produced for the Brazilian Army

Jiefang CA-30A **China**

The prototype of the **Jiefang CA-30** was produced in 1958 with the design based on the **Soviet ZIL-157 unit.**.

Production did not commence until 1964 at the Ch'ang-Ch'un Motor Vehicle Manufacturing Plant in Jilin Province. The first production versions used the cab of the Jiefang **CA-10** (see next entry), together with touches that differentiate the CA-30 from the ZIL-157. Early models had a 95 hp petrol engine but this was later changed to the more powerful 115 hp engine. The later **CA-30A** differed from the earlier CA-30 by the addition of a front-mounted winch; it appears that all **CA-30As** have the more powerful engine. The CA-30 and **CA-30A** became the standard 2.5 tonne load-carrying truck of the People's Liberation Army and many were exported to nations such as North VietNam.

Variants are numerous and many for the CA-30 series was used for virtually every military purpose conceivable from light artillery tractor to multiple rocket launcher and from drilling truck to truck tractors and buses. Perhaps the most unusual variant resembles a multiple rocket launcher but is used to launch the Type 74 land minelaying rocket system. Body styles vary accordingly but the most common version is the open cargo-carrying version with slatted sides and capable of carrying up to 4,500 kg on roads; towed loads of up to 3,600 kg can be towed across country and troops can be carried on folding bench seats.

Many CA-30s are also used by civilian organisations. At one period up to 7,000 CA-30s were produced every year but production ceased during 1986.

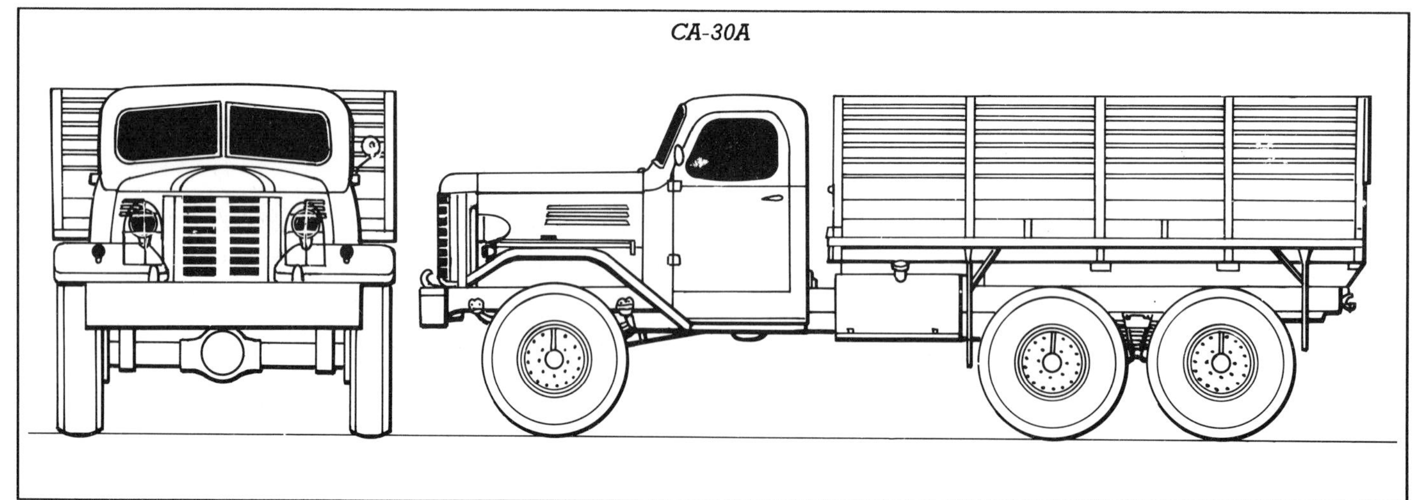
CA-30A

Specification

Role: general utility truck and artillery tractor
Cab seating: 1 + 2
Configuration: 6 x 6
Weight: (empty) 5450 kg
Max load: 2500 kg
Length: 6.922 m
Width: 2.315 m
Height: 2.36 m
Ground clearance: 0.305 m

Track: 1.752 m
Wheelbase: 4.785 m
Max speed: (road) 65 km/h
Fuel capacity: 150 litres
Fording: 0.85 m
Engine: Chieh'Fang 120 5.5 litre 6-cylinder petrol
Power output: 115 hp/2800 rpm
Gearbox: manual, 5f, 1r

Clutch: single dry plate
Transfer box: 2-speed
Steering: mechanical
Turning circle: 24.2 m
Suspension: leaf springs
Tyres: 12.00 x 18
Electrical system: 12 V

Variants: CA-30, CA-30A, also see text

Chinese Army CA-30 6 x 6 truck towing 122 mm howitzer

Tatra T 815

Czechoslovakia

The **Tatra T 815** is the latest production version of the earlier **Tatra 813**. Both are named **'Kolos'** and are large and powerful load carriers produced in both 6 x 6 and 8 x 8 versions. There are two versions of the 8 x 8, one having a two- door cab, the other having four doors (with internal space for at least one bunk). The 6 x 6 version has a payload capacity of 8,000 kg.

The **Tatra 815** follows the earlier version in using a frameless chassis with the load-bearing section using main assembly unit cases inter-connected by load bearing tubes. The forward control cab is mounted on a through-frame to which all other forward components, including the engine, are fitted. In its cargo form, the Tatra **T 815** is used to carry heavy loads across country in forward areas but the vehicle is also used to carry heavy combat engineer equipment such as floating bridge sections. It is also used to carry the Czech 122 mm RM-70/85 multiple (40-round) rocket system and the basic 8 x 8 chassis is used as the basis of the 152 mm Dana self-propelled howitzer.

The basic cargo version is also used as an artillery tractor for calibres up to 152 mm. Most versions carry a self-recovery winch and add-on extras include snow ploughs and a dozer blade for clearing obstacles. One special engineer version carries a large crane and a dozer blade. A tyre pressure regulation system may be fitted. The Tatra **813** and **T 815** have been exported and the 6 x 6 version of the **T 815** is licence-produced in India; the 8 x 8 version is used by the Indian Army.

A 4 x 4 version was introduced during 1993.

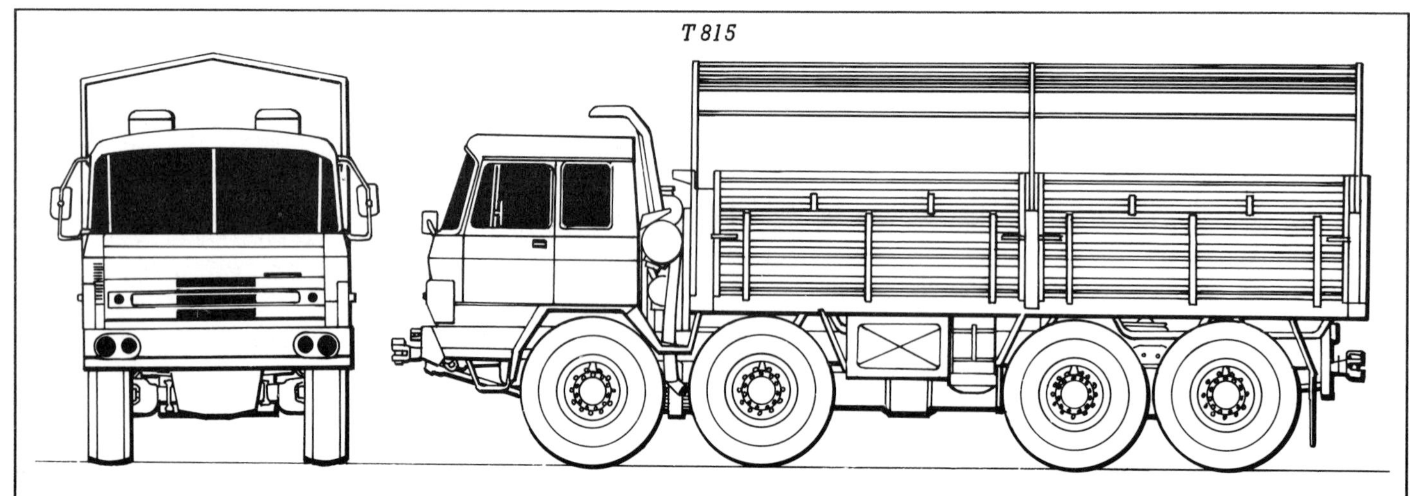
T 815

Specification

Role: heavy utility truck and artillery tractor
Cab seating: 1 + 3 or 5
Configuration: 8 x 8
Weight: (empty) 15,100 kg
Max load: 15,000 kg
Length: 9.36 m
Width: 2.5 m
Height: 3.65 m
Ground clearance: 0.41 m
Track: 2.044 m/1.988 m
Wheelbase: 1.65 m + 2.97 m + 1.45 m
Max speed: (road) 80 km/h
Fuel capacity: 460 litres
Fording: 1.4 m
Engine: 3-930-50 19 litre V-12 diesel
Power output: 347 hp/2200 rpm
Gearbox: manual, 10f, 2r
Clutch: triple dry plate
Transfer box: 2-speed
Steering: worm and roller, power assisted
Turning circle: n/av
Suspension: leaf springs and shock absorbers
Tyres: 15.00-21 TO3
Electrical system: 24 V

Variants: see text

Tatra T 815 truck as licence produced in India by Bharat Earth Movers Limited (BEML)

Sisu SA-110 VS

Finland

The **Sisu SA-110 VS** is the production successor to the **Sisu A-45**, a 4 x 4 3-tonne truck still in widespread service with the Finnish armed forces (and United Nations peace - keeping units). Both trucks are extremely tough for they were designed to carry out forward area supply duties under harsh Finnish winter and terrain conditions and thus have a good cross country performance . The **SA-110 VS** therefore features a high ground clearance (0.57 m) and uses a heavy coil spring suspension for the front axle.

To date only one version appears to have been produced, a cargo carrier with a distinctive all-steel forward control cab and an all-steel load-carrying area. The cargo area can be covered by a tarpaulin and may have full length or partial drop sides and a tailgate. There is provision to fit bench seating for troops along each side. A towing hitch for trailers or light artillery weapons is fitted at the rear. The usual power plant is a Valmet 144 hp diesel but it is possible to install a Deutz 160 hp diesel.

Other options include a self-recovery 3,500 kg winch and an add-on armour kit for the cab.

An optional central tyre pressure regulation system controlled from the cab can improve traction across soft ground and snow.

It is anticipated that the **SA-110 VS** will assume many of the roles currently carried out by the **Sisu A-45** so there may eventually be ambulance, fire and crash tender, radio, workshop and command variants.

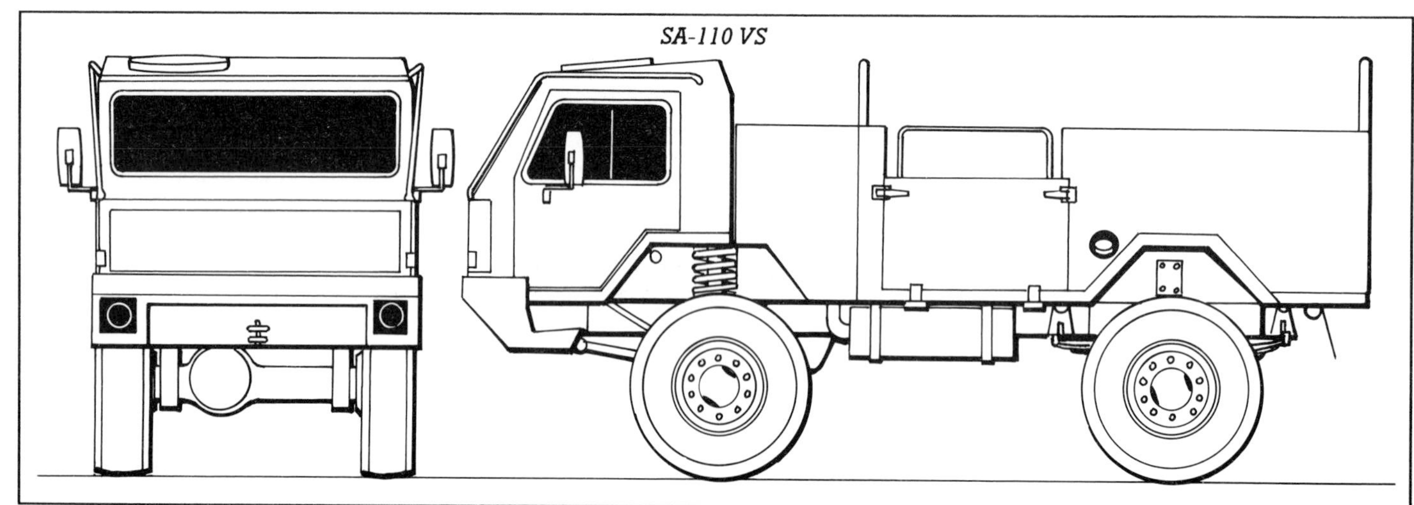

Specification

Role: forward area utility truck
Cab seating: 1 + 2
Configuration: 4 x 4
Weight: (empty) 5950 kg
Max load: 3550 kg
Length: 6.5 m
Width: 2.34 m
Height: 2.84 m
Ground clearance: 0.57 m
Track: n/av
Wheelbase: 3.4 m
Max speed: (road) 100 km/h
Fuel capacity: 165 litres
Fording: 0.9 m
Engine: Valmet 411 DSJ diesel
Power output: 144 hp/2500 rpm
Gearbox: ZF S 5.35/2 manual, 5f, 1r
Clutch: single dry plate
Transfer box: Sisu 2-speed
Steering: hydraulic, power assisted
Turning circle: approx 16 m
Suspension: front, coil springs; rear leaf springs: both with shock absorbers
Tyres: 14.00 x 20
Electrical system: 24 V

Variants: see text

Sisu SA-110 VS 4 x 4 3.5-tonne truck

Renault TRM 2000

Production of the **Renault TRM 2000** commenced during 1983 and manufactures at a rate of about 140 vehicles each month - at one time the French Army had a requirement for 12,000 of these vehicles but this total may not be achieved due to defence budget restrictions.

The **TRM 2000** uses a forward control cab layout and two main versions are produced. One is the High Mobility model with the other being a straight axle model having reduced ground clearances (0.302 m) under the axle differentials and with a reduced overall height (2.59 m). Both models are otherwise identical. The usual forward-tilting hard-topped cab can be replaced by a soft-top version known as a 'torpedo' cab. This version is normally used completely open as it is intended for use in North Africa and has been procured by Morocco. The overall construction of the **TRM 2000** is extremely strong and it has an excellent cross country performance. When used as a personnel transporter, bench seats can be erected in the rear to carry up to 12 troops. The drop sides and tailgate can be removed to enable the vehicle to carry communication and other shelters while van-bodied versions can be used as ambulances or command posts.

There is also a 2000-litre tanker version, a specialised forward air control post for strike aircraft and the vehicle has been used to carry 20 mm anti-aircraft cannon fired from the load area. It can also be used to tow 120 mm mortars or trailers weighing up to 2000 kg.

Recovery vehicle and workshop vehicle variants have been produced.

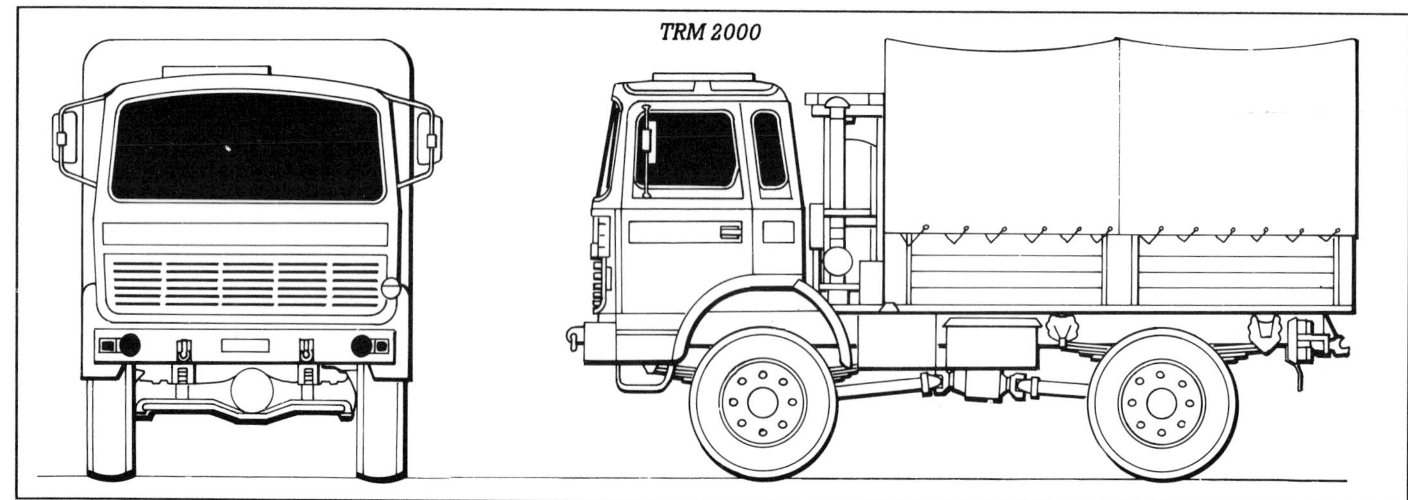

Specification

Role: light utility vehicle
Cab seating: 1 + 2
Configuration: 4 x 4
Weight: (empty) 3980 kg
Max load: 2320 kg
Length: 5.02 m
Width: 2.2 m
Height: 2.713 m
Ground clearance: 0.425 m
Track: 1.8 m
Wheelbase: 2.7 m
Max speed: (road) 89 km/h
Fuel capacity: 130 litres
Fording: 0.9 m
Engine: Renault type 720 S Pc 3.595 litre 4-cylinder supercharged diesel
Power output: 117 hp/3000 rpm
Gearbox: Type S 5-24/3 manual, 5f, 1r
Clutch: Type 250 DBR single dry plate
Transfer box: 2-speed
Steering: ball race, hydraulic power assisted
Turning circle: 14 m
Suspension: leaf springs and shock absorbers
Tyres: 12.50 x 20
Electrical system: 24 V

Variants: see text

Renault TRM 2000 4 x 4 truck acting as tractor vehicle for 20 mm light anti-aircraft gun

Renault TRM 4000 France

The **Renault TRM 4000** was a military development of the commercial **Saviem SM8** truck. When production commenced in 1973 it was intended that the **TRM 4000** would become the French armed forces' standard vehicle in its class. At that time there was stated to be a requirement for 15,000 of these vehicles but production ceased at Blainville during the late 1980s before even half this total had been achieved.

The **TRM 4000** made extensive use of proven commercial components (such as the engine, transmission, chassis frame and axles) and is conventional in layout, using a modified **Saviem/Renault Type 812** forward control two-door cab fitted with a roof hatch. Optionally it may be split at door level for air transport.

The standard version is a conventional cargo carrier but many other versions were, and still are, in French Army service; some were exported to undisclosed countries in North Africa.

One version uses a van-type body that can be configured internally for use as anything from an ambulance to a mobile office or workshop. Another version, now withdrawn, was used as a Crotale missile carrier and was equipped with a hydraulic crane. Cranes are also used on a light recovery vehicle and a specialised crane truck.

Numerous fire tender bodies have been developed and there are fuel and water tanker versions. There is also a dump truck version.

Some vehicles have a front-mounted winch while others have a 200 litre fuel tank and extra fuel can racks.

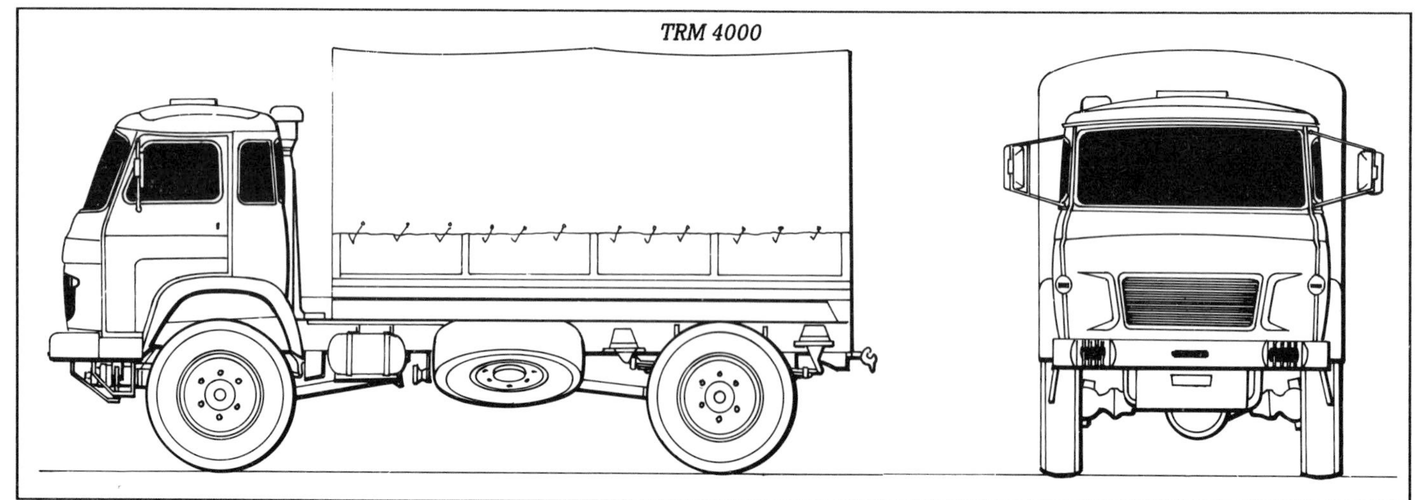

Specification

Role: medium utility truck
Cab seating: 1 + 1
Configuration: 4 x 4
Weight: (empty) 5680 kg
Max load: 4320 kg
Length: 6.538 m
Width: 2.19 m
Height: 2.75 m
Ground clearance: 0.28 m
Track: 1.836 m/2.018 m
Wheelbase: 3.85 m
Max speed: (road) 87 km/h
Fuel capacity: 150 litres
Fording: 0.9 m
Engine: Renault Type 797 5.491 litre 6-cylinder diesel
Power output: 133 hp/2900 rpm
Gearbox: Type ET 301 manual, 5f, 1r
Clutch: Type 12 LF 45 single dry plate
Transfer box: Type G 300 2-speed
Steering: cam and roller
Turning circle: 20 m
Suspension: leaf springs and pads plus shock absorbers
Tyres: 12.00 x 20
Electrical system: 24 V

Variants: see text

Renault TRM 4000 4 x 4 truck carrying air defence radar

Renault TRM 10 000

Production of the **Renault TRM 10 000** (*le 'dix mille'*) commenced at Blainville during 1985. It is a development of the earlier **Renault TRM 9000** 9 tonne truck which was developed primarily for export. The **TRM 10 000** differs by having a longer wheelbase, a revised transmission and a more powerful engine.

The initial order was for 178 vehicles and a second order for 759 was placed in 1987. It is understood that the French Army requirement is 5,000 vehicles but indications are that this total may not be reached.

The **TRM 10 000** is a large and powerful vehicle with a box-like forward control cab and a large load-carrying area. It is produced in several forms for it is used by the French Army to carry out several roles. It is used as a load carrier, with or without a hydraulic crane, and some vehicles have an enlarged four-door cab to accommodate up to four passengers or crew bunks. Up to 24 troops can be carried on benches in the cargo area.

There is an artillery tractor version used to tow the **155 mm TR** gun; this version has the enlarged crew cab.

A tractor truck version is used to tow PFM floating bridge sections while one special version is used to carry a large Tropomil data link system dish aerial. There is a missile system resupply vehicle used to carry spare missiles a heavy recovery version and a dump truck.

Other versions such as tankers are under development.

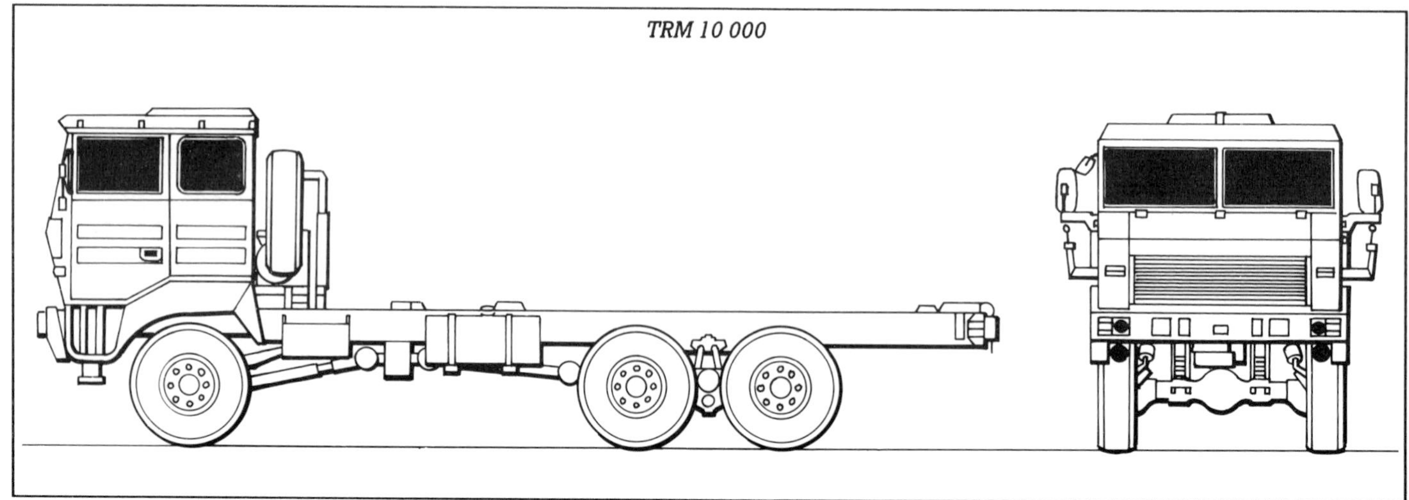

TRM 10 000

Specification

Role: heavy utility truck and artillery tractor
Cab seating: 1 + 1 or 2
Configuration: 6 x 6
Weight: (empty) 10,290 kg
Max load: 10,000 kg
Length: (cab and chassis) 9.246 m
Width: 2.48 m
Height: 3.11 m
Ground clearance: 0.382 m
Track: 2.004 m/2.053 m
Wheelbase: 4.3 m + 1.4 m
Max speed: (road) 89 km/h
Fuel capacity: 500 litres
Fording: 1.2 m
Engine: Renault Type MIDS 06.20.45 9.839 litre 6-cylinder supercharged diesel
Power output: 264 hp/2200 rpm
Gearbox: Type B.9.150 manual, 9f, 1r
Clutch: Type 430 DPT 2400
Transfer box: Type A 800 3 D 2-speed
Steering: Type 8046 power assisted
Turning circle: 21 m
Suspension: leaf springs with mechanical stops and shock absorbers at front
Tyres: 14.00 x 20
Electrical system: 24 V

Variants: see text

Renault TRM 10 000 configured as ammunition carrier with hydraulic crane at rear

The ACMAT VLRA Trucks

France

The **ACMAT** trucks have been in production since the late 1950s and display a remarkable degree of commonality and inter-changeability between all the many models.

Produced by *Ateliers de Construction Mecanique de l'Atlantique* (hence **ACMAT**) the truck range is known as the **VLRA** - *Vehicule de Liason, de Reconnaissance et d'Appui* - and encompasses a wide range of vehicles from a 4 x 4 field car up to 6 x 6 tractor trucks. There is even an 8 x 8 load carrier. All these vehicles have identical detail design commonality and parts from any vehicle can be used on any other, no matter what its age, size or role. Thus each **ACMAT** truck uses the same engine mounting brackets, the same tyres, the same door handles, and so on.

Each model is an uncompromising military vehicle and is delivered complete with a 200 litre water tank and a kit of spares and tools.

The range includes construction vehicles, missile carriers, a rocket launcher, buses, ambulances, crane vehicles, armed patrol vehicles, an armoured personnel carrier, command vehicles, shelter carriers, workshop vehicles, and so on.

The overall design of the **ACMAT** trucks has remained unaltered since the late 1950s although some changes have been made to accommodate improvements in components, but the mounting arrangements for those components remains unchanged.

Cabs are usually open or soft-topped but hard-tops and crew cabs are available. It has been claimed that **ACMAT** are now the only military truck producers in the world for any commercial sales involve military vehicle designs only.

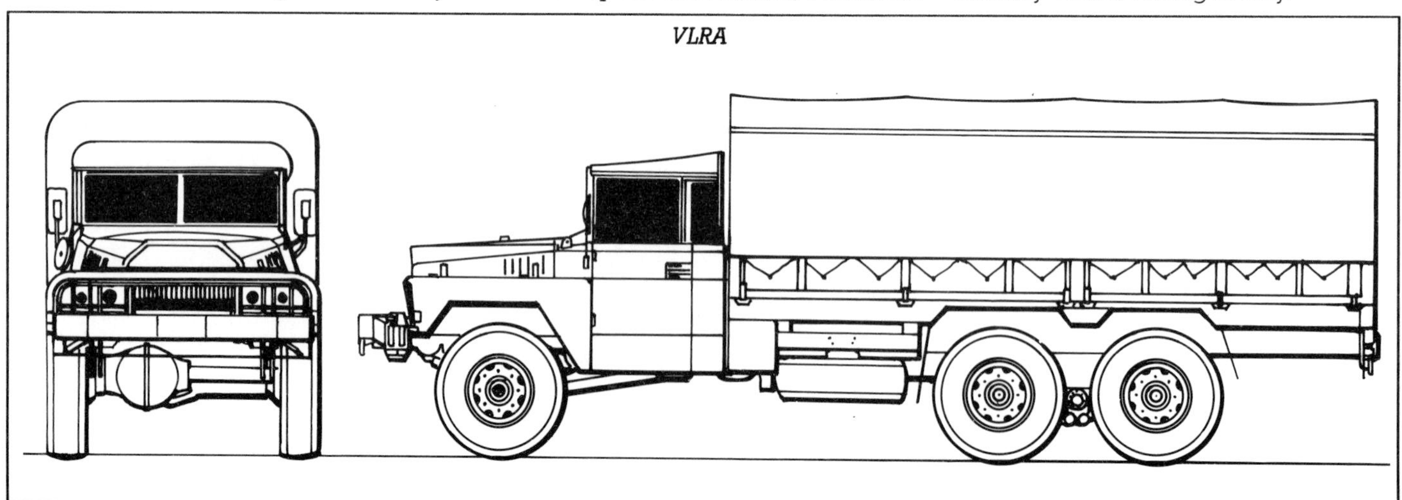
VLRA

Specification

TPK 4.20 SM3

Role: general utility vehicle
Cab seating: 1 + 2
Configuration: 4 x 4
Weight: (empty) 4300 kg
Max load: 2500 kg
Length: 6 m
Width: 2.07 m
Height: 2.62 m
Ground clearance: 0.287 m
Track: 1.76 m/1.66 m
Wheelbase: 3.6 m
Max speed: (road) 100 km/h
Fuel capacity: 360 litres
Fording: 0.9 m
Engine: Perkins 6.354.4 6-cylinder diesel
Power output: 120 hp/2800 rpm
Gearbox: Type 435 manual, 4f, 1r
Clutch: Type 12 L 35 single dry plate
Transfer box: ACMAT 2-speed
Steering: worm and nut
Turning circle: 17 m
Suspension: leaf springs and shock absorbers
Tyres: 12.5 x 20 XL
Electrical system: 24 V

Variants: Many - see text

ACMAT VLRA TPK 4.15 SM3 4 x 4 truck carrying light artillery rocket system

Berliet GBC 8 KT

France

The **Berliet GBC 8 KT** had its origins in a commercial design known as the **Gazelle** which was developed specifically for use in North Africa. A series of modifications resulted in the military **GBC 8 KT** which was ordered for the French armed forces and was subsequently exported to nations such as Portugal and Algeria. The type was also licence-produced in China. By the time production was completed over 18,000 had been produced and the type remains a standard French armed forces vehicle.

The vehicle has a distinctive bonnet shape and is normally seen with a removable soft top to the cab.

The base vehicle is a conventional load carrier with the usual tilt covering the load area but the type is frequently used as a flat bed carrier for a variety of communications and other shelters or electrical generators and air compressors.

There are a number of variants. The KT series has a multi-fuel engine while the MT series uses a conventional 150 hp diesel. There is a 4 x 4 variant, which was sold to Algeria and Portugal, and a long wheelbase (3.71 m + 1.28 m) model with increased dimensions overall.

Some vehicles have winches and/or hydraulic loading cranes. Two types of recovery vehicle are still used and there are 5000-litre tanker, tipper truck and fire tender versions. There is also a tractor truck used to tow specialised semi-trailers and aircraft refueller versions.

Plans are being made to modernise these trucks by installing a new engine, cab and other components.

Berliet is now part of Renault Véhicules Industriels (RVI).

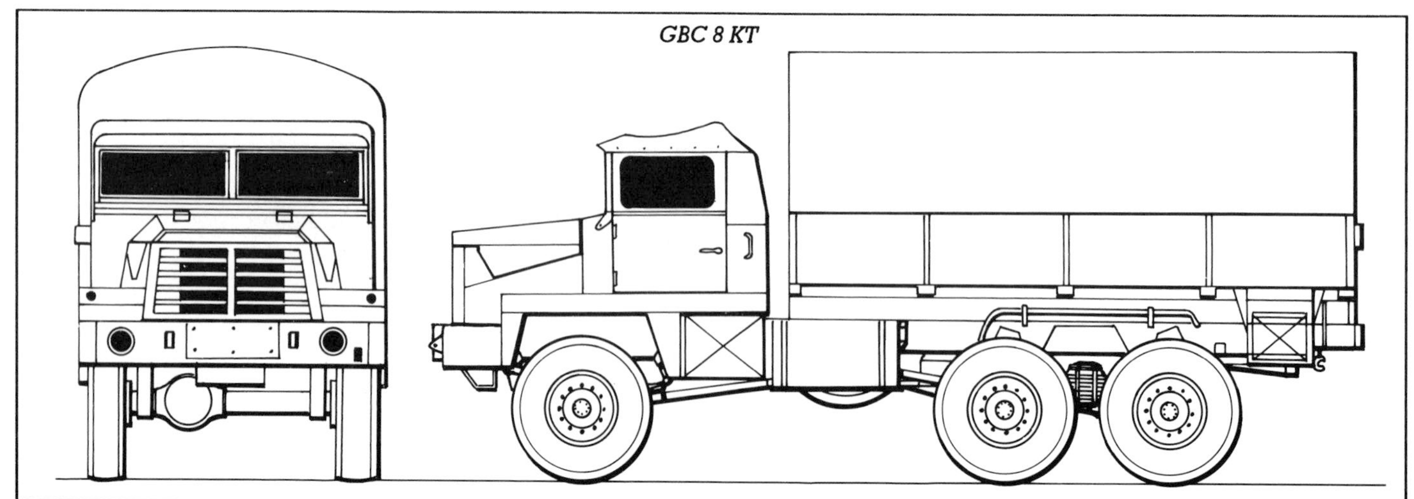
GBC 8 KT

Specification

Role: general utility truck
Cab seating: 1 + 2
Configuration: 6 x 6
Weight: (empty) 8370 kg
Max load: 4000 kg
Length: 7.28 m
Width: 2.4 m
Height: 3.3 m
Ground clearance: 0.28 m
Track: 1.86 m
Wheelbase: 3.31 m + 1.28 m
Max speed: (road) 80 km/h
Fuel capacity: 200 litres
Fording: 1.2 m
Engine: Berliet MK 520 7.9 litre, 5 cylinder multi-fuel
Power output: 125 hp/2100 rpm
Gearbox: Berliet BDSL 13 manual, 6f, 1r
Clutch: single dry plate
Transfer box: 2-speed
Steering: worm and nut
Turning circle: 21 m
Suspension: leaf springs and shock absorbers
Tyres: 12.00 x 20
Electrical system: 24 V

Variants: see text

Berliet GBC 8 KT 6 x 6 4-tonne truck configured as fire tender

The Unimogs

The first **Unimog** (*Universal Motor Gerät*) was designed in 1946 and the prototypes were first shown during 1948. Ever since then the **Unimog** range has been expanded to encompass a family of 4 x 4 general utility trucks with off-road payloads of between 1250 and 5000 kg.

Over the years many models have been introduced and body styles have altered considerably but the basic design has remained constant. All versions are tough and efficient vehicles with excellent cross country performance capabilities. There are varying wheelbases, engine capacities and outputs, load area dimensions and many other variables to ensure that there is a **Unimog** to meet any particular military logistics requirement.

The smallest model is the **U 600 L** and the largest the **U 1700 L**, although a recent redesignation system has been introduced to include even more wheelbase lengths and payload capacities. There is also a 6 x 6 **Unimog**, the **U2150 L** with an 8000 kg capacity. All these models are entirely conventional, using strong ladder-frame chassis with torsional flexibility and a coil spring suspension. The all-steel cab has a roll-over safety feature and the entire cab and bonnet can be tilted forward for maintenance. Apart from the usual cargo body model there are ambulance, communications, command, trench-digging, workshop and fire tender versions and the **Unimog** are frequently used to carry snow ploughs and other attachments such as front-mounted fork lifts. **Unimogs** are also used as light artillery tractors. **Unimogs** have been exported to all over the world and they are licence-produced in Australia.

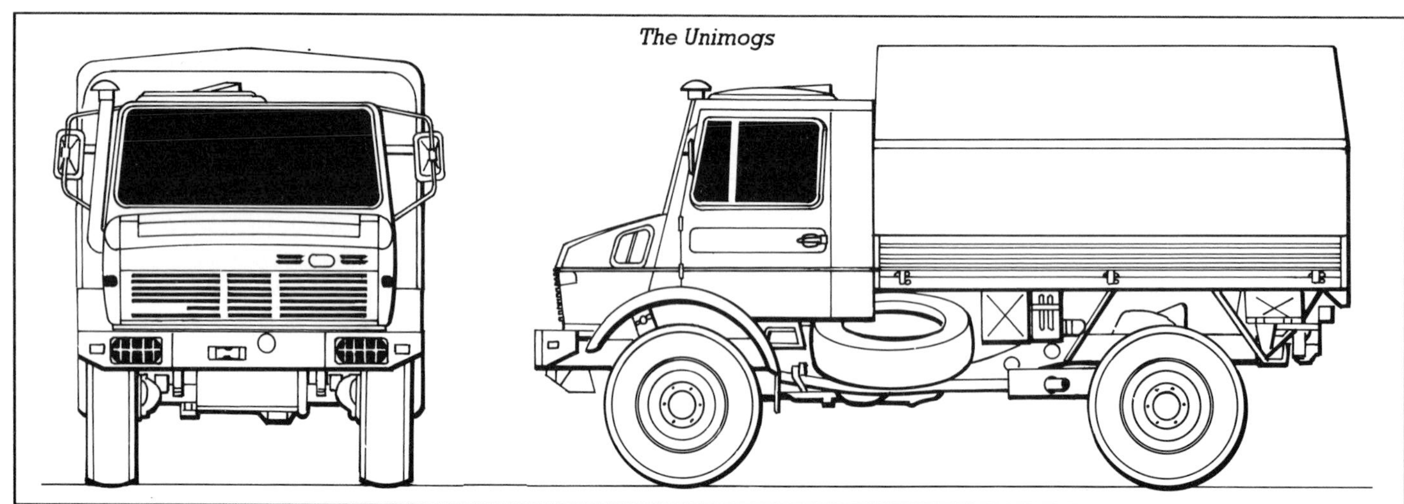

The Unimogs

Specification

U 1300 L

Role: general utility truck
Cab seating: 1 + 1
Configuration: 4 x 4
Weight: (empty) 5000 kg
Max load: 2250 kg
Length: 5.555 m
Width: 2.32 m
Height: 2.8 m
Ground clearance: 0.44 m
Track: 1.86 m
Wheelbase: 3.25 m
Max speed: (road) 82 km/h
Fuel capacity: 160 litres
Fording: 1.2 m
Engine: MB OM 352 5.675 litre 6 cylinder diesel
Power output: 130 hp/2800 rpm
Gearbox: UG 3/40 manual 8f, 8r
Clutch: single dry plate
Transfer box: 2-speed
Steering: hydraulic power assisted
Turning circle: approx 14 m
Suspension: coil springs and telescopic shock absorbers
Tyres: 12.5 R 20
Electrical system: 12 or 24 V

Variants: Many, see text

New Zealand Army Unimog U 1300 L 4 x 4 truck

IVECO Magirus 120-19 ANWM **Germany**

The **IVECO Magirus 120-19 ANWM** was originally designated the **Magirus Deutz 192D 12AL**, the designation changed during the mid-1980s when Magirus Deutz became part of the Industrial Vehicles Corporation (IVECO) consortium. It is an enlarged version of the 4000 kg **90-13 ANWM** and follows the same general lines in having a prominent squared-off bonnet, a hard-topped military style sound-proofed cab with an optional roof hatch, and an all-steel cargo area at the rear which can be covered by the usual canvas tilt over removable bows.

Provision is made for folding bench seating for up to 18 troops in the cargo area. Securing points for shelters and logistic containers are provided. Prominent air intake ducts extend each side of the one-piece windscreen. These ducts come into prominence when a special wading kit for depths up to 1.2 metres is fitted.

Other optional equipment includes an enlarged fuel tank (200 litres) or the same-sized additional tank to extend range even further (ie 200 + 130 litres).

A 5000 or 7000 kg mechanical or hydraulic winch may be fitted. If required a power take-off on the transfer case can be utilised to drive power tools. As usual, the **120-19 ANWM** can be used to accommodate a variety of body types including ambulances, tippers, recovery rigs, van bodies and tankers. The type is also used as an artillery tractor.

The **120-19 ANWM** was apparently used as the starting point for the design of the South African **SAMIL 50** (qv).

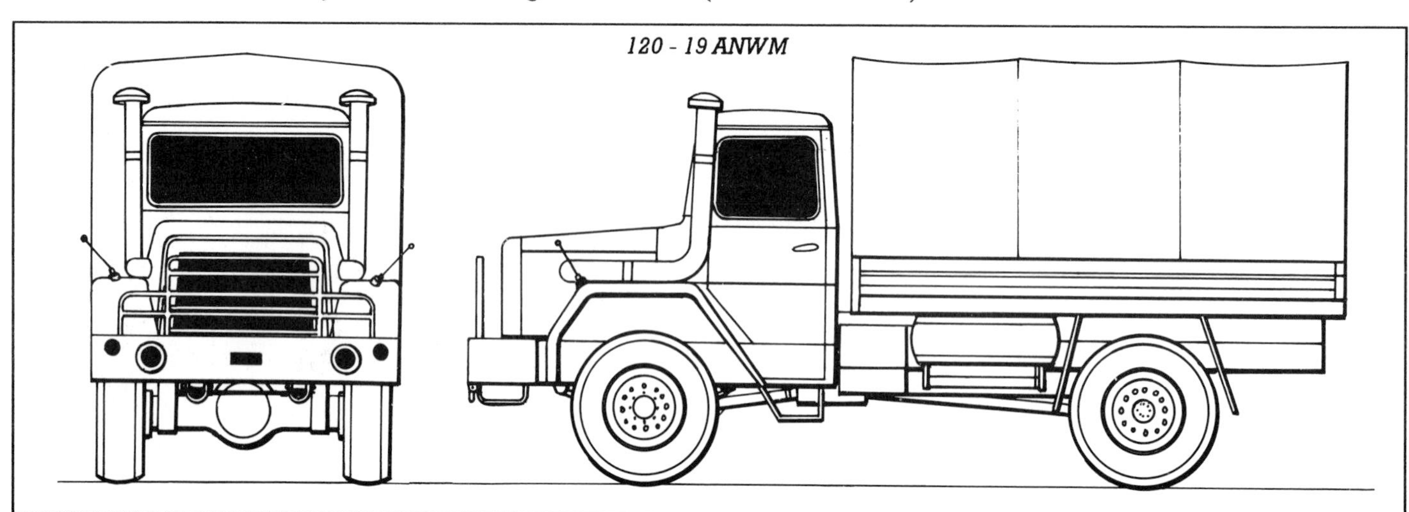
120 - 19 ANWM

Specification

Role: general utility truck
Cab seating: 1 + 2
Configuration: 4 x 4
Weight: (empty) 7300 kg
Max load: 5000 kg
Length: 8.405 m
Width: 2.5 m
Height: 3.38 m
Ground clearance: 0.37 m
Track: 1.985 m/2.03 m
Wheelbase: 4.9 m
Max speed: (road) 85 km/h
Fuel capacity: 130 litres
Fording: 0.8 m
Engine: Deutz Diesel F6L 413 9.572 litre 6 cylinder diesel
Power output: 192 hp/2500 rpm
Gearbox: manual, 6f, 1r
Clutch: single dry plate
Transfer box: 2-speed
Steering: ball and nut, power assisted
Turning circle: 24 m
Suspension: leaf springs with shock absorbers
Tyres: 14.00 x 20
Electrical system: 24 V

Variants: see text

IVECO Magirus 120-19 ANWM truck with stowage platform over cab

MAN 11.136 HA

Germany/Belgium

The **MAN 11.136 HA** is another example of proven commercial components and an existing commercial design being combined to produce a viable and efficient military general utility truck at a relatively low cost compared to custom-designing.

In 1975 the Belgian Ministry of Defence ordered 3000 of these vehicles which were subsequently produced by MAN in kit form and assembled in Belgium by MAN importers Hocke. A later order placed in 1981 involved a number of similar 4 x 2 trucks designated the **11.136 H**, some of which were delivered in tipper truck form. The **11.136 HA** trucks are entirely conventional vehicles that can be recognised by their distinctive curved bonnet cowls. Most vehicles are used as straightforward 5000 kg cargo trucks with the timber-floored cargo area covered by a tilt over curved bows, but many variants in bodywork exist.

The steel-sided cargo area can be used to carry shelters and/or containers. Van bodies for command, workshop and office purposes are widely used along with refrigerated van-bodied mobile larder vehicles.

There are several types of fuel tanker, some for aircraft refuelling purposes and others for field refuelling armoured vehicles. A towing hitch at the rear allows light artillery weapons or trailers to be towed.

The **11.136 HA** truck has been replaced on the German production lines by a later model, the 4 x 4 **MAN 14.240 HAE**; some have been exported to North African armed forces.

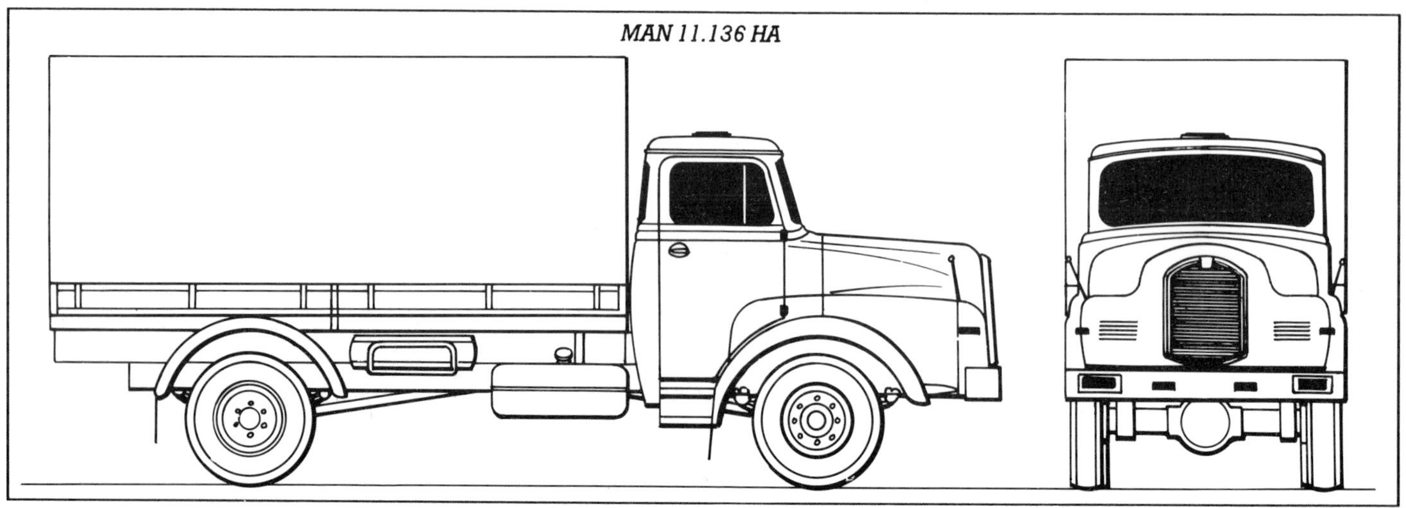

MAN 11.136 HA

Specification

Role: general utility truck
Cab seating: 1 + 2
Configuration: 4 x 4
Weight: (empty) 6000 kg
Max load: 5000 kg
Length: 7.305 m
Width: 2.3 m
Height: 2.605 m
Ground clearance: 0.33 m
Track: 1.82 m/1.664 m
Wheelbase: 4.4 m
Max speed: (road) 84 km/h
Fuel capacity: 200 litres
Fording: 0.75 m
Engine: MAN/Renault Model 797/06 5.5 litre 6 cylinder diesel
Power output: 150 hp/3000 rpm
Gearbox: ZF S 5-35 manual, 5f, 1r
Clutch: single dry plate
Transfer box: G 300 2-speed
Steering: ZF Gemmer worm and roller
Turning circle: 19.3 m
Suspension: leaf springs with rubber springs
Tyres: 9.00 x 20
Electrical system: 24 V

Variants: 11.136 HA, 11.136 H

Belgian Army MAN 11.136 HA 5-tonne truck

The MAN High Mobility Tactical Trucks Germany

The **MAN High Mobility Tactical Truck** range includes 4 x 4, 6 x 6,, and 8 x 8 trucks. They all stem from a (then) West German Army staff requirement drawn up during the early 1960s - production began during 1976. Ever since then these trucks have rolled off the Salzgitter-Watenstedt lines in thousands and by the end of 1984 the German armed forces had accepted over 14,000 units and thousands more have since been exported.

All models share a common cab and many other components including a low torsion chassis frame, axles and suspension. Many components have commercial origins. The end result is a range of powerful multi-purpose trucks that are uncompromisingly military in appearance and function. On all models the same forward tilting and forward control all-steel cab is used. The basic cargo body is an open all-steel unit and material handling cranes are widely used - a winch is also a standard item.

The trucks are used for just about any military purpose possible and there is even a special wide version (2.9 m) of the 8 x 8 for carrying shelters and other loads requiring high stability; this chassis is used to carry the Roland air defence missile system. Load handling systems are frequently used in place of the usual cargo area, handling everything from ammunition flatracks to floating bridge sections. Special applications include carrying telescopic masts and other equipment for the Patriot missile system, and elevating combat platforms for anti-tank missile systems. Recovery and fire/crash tender versions have been produced.

The US armed forces have used these trucks to support cruise missile units. Licence-built examples have been produced in Austria by **OAF**. Optional equipment includes an armoured cab.

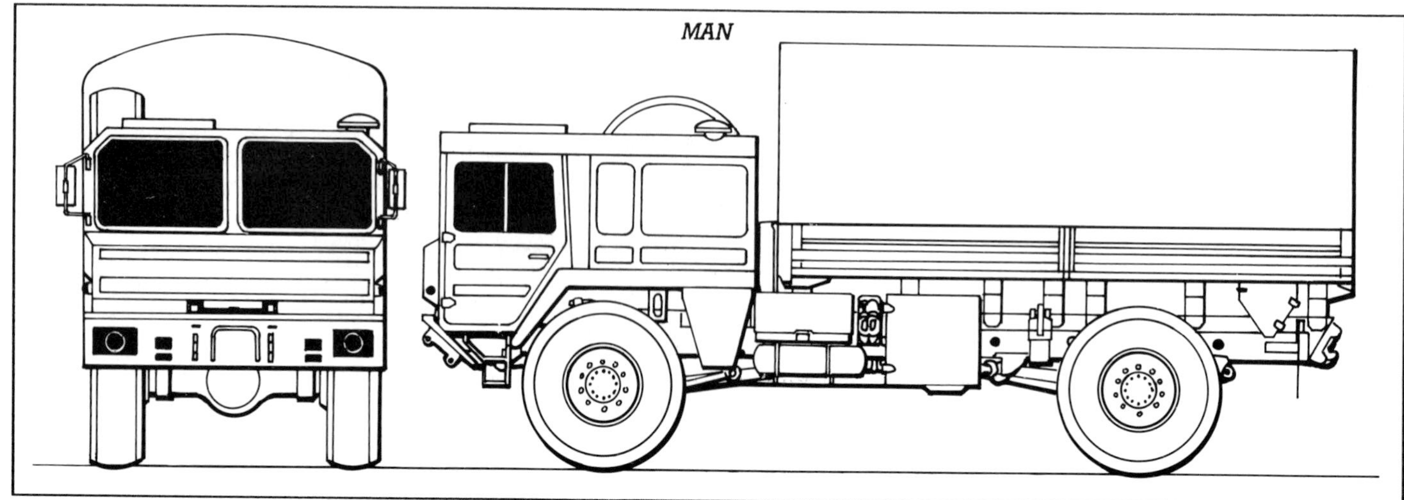

Specification

8 x 8 version

Role: general utility and logistics trucks
Cab seating: 1 + 2
Configuration: 8 x 8
Weight: (empty) 13,400 kg
Max load: up to 16,000 kg
Length: 10.27 m
Width: 2.5 m
Height: 2.93 m
Ground clearance: 0.41 m
Track: 2.07 m
Wheelbase: 1.93 m + 3.57 m + 1.5 m
Max speed: (road) 90 km/h
Fuel capacity: 400 litres
Fording: 1.2 m
Engine: MAN D 2866 KFG 6 cylinder diesel
Power output: 360 hp/2200 rpm
Gearbox: ZF series, up to 16f, 2r
Clutch: converter
Transfer box: 2-speed
Steering: recirculating ball, power assisted
Turning circle: 27.4 m
Suspension: rigid axles, helical springs
Tyres: 14.00 R 20 or 16.00 R 20
Electrical system: 24 V

Variants: see text

MAN 6 x 6 High Mobility Tactical Truck

MAN 415 L1 AR/Shaktiman Germany/India

The **MAN 415 L1 AR** was a progressive development of the earlier **MAN 400 L1 E**, a 3-tonne truck, and shared many chassis and cab components. Some were produced for use by the German armed forces but the main bulk of the units produced were (and still are) manufactured in India by the Vehicle Factory at Jabalpur. The Indian version is known as the **Shaktiman** and differs from the German original mainly in having dual tyres at the rear (instead of the original single tyres).

The first Shaktimans appeared during 1958 and used components supplied from MAN but later versions featured an ever-increasing number of locally-produced parts. Early models had 100 hp engines; output has been increased to 110 hp and special versions are produced for use at altitude and in desert conditions. Both 4 x 4 and 4 x 2 versions are available. Shaktimans are used by the Indian Army and many Indian police forces and may have either hard or soft-topped cabs. The cargo area is frequently left open but can be covered by a canvas tilt. Bench seats for troops are a common fitment. An amphibious version known as the **Rampar** and with a 3-tonne payload (or 22 men) was produced for extended trials during the mid-1970s. A development has a deeper chassis frame, a heavy duty suspension and larger tyres; it has a maximum payload of up to 6000 kg. One version of the basic Shaktiman is used as a tractor for 105 mm field guns. Back in Germany gradual development resulted in the **MAN 630** series which were larger overall and have a 5 tonne payload. Many of these remain in service in Belgium (locally assembled as the **MAN 630 L2 AE-B**) and West Germany. The 630 series is now out of production.

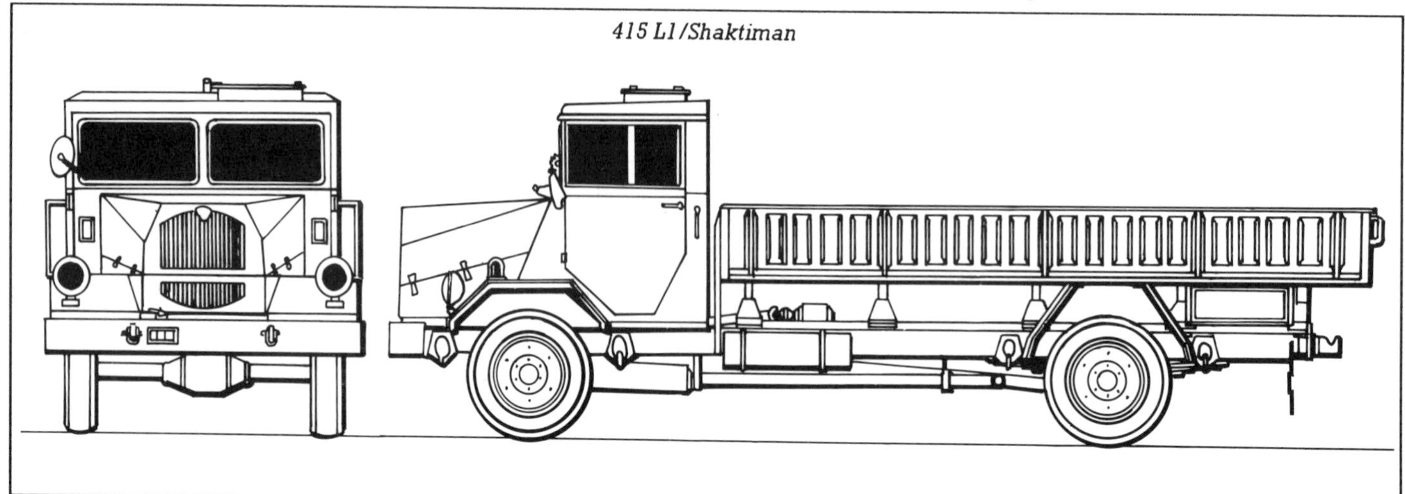

415 L1/Shaktiman

Specification

Role: general utility truck
Cab seating: 1 + 1 or 2
Configuration: 4 x 4
Weight: (empty) 5193 kg
Max load: approx 4000 kg
Length: 7.16 m
Width: 2.35 m
Height: 2.435 m
Ground clearance: 0.308 m
Track: 1.824 m/1.632 m
Wheelbase: 4.2 m
Max speed: (road) approx 70 km/h
Fuel capacity: 300 litres
Fording: 0.8 m
Engine: D 0026 M 8 A 5.88 litre 6 cylinder diesel
Power output: 110 hp/2500 rpm
Gearbox: AK5-35 manual, 5f, 1r
Clutch: single dry plate
Transfer box: 2-speed
Steering: heavy duty roller
Turning circle: 16.15 m
Suspension: leaf springs
Tyres: 8.25 x 20-12 ply
Electrical system: 12 V

Variants: see text

MAN 415 series 4 x 4 truck retained by the Luftwaffe as a mobile office

M-325 Commandcar

The **M-325 Commandcar** is one of the Israeli armed forces' standard vehicles and is used in several forms. The first Commandcar was produced during 1966, based on a Dodge Power Wagon model and making use of many standard and readily-available components that were assembled at the Automotive Industries plant at Nazareth Illit. Thus the axles were Dana Spicer, the engine from Chrysler, the transfer box from New Process, the steering gear from Ross, disc brakes from Bendix, and so on. The end result has proved to be an extremely tough and adaptable vehicle.

The base model is a cargo and personnel carrier with a pvc- covered tarpaulin protecting up to 12 troops in the rear area. This version is also used to tow a trailer or 120 mm mortar, or carry a communications shelter. A patrol and reconnaissance model for use in combat areas has machine gun and spotlight pintles and there is provision to carry a 1300 litre fuel or water tank.

Van bodies can be used as the basis for an ambulance or a command vehicle.

There is also an open mine-protected version with a strengthened floor, prominent roll bars and special seating for eight troops in the rear. The seats can be removed when cargo is carried. At one time a light armoured personnel carrier version was under development.

The most unusual variant is a mobile airfield control cabin with the cabin elevated to a height of 6.5 m when in use.

The Commandcar has been exported (one known customer is Peru) with optional equipment such as a 98 hp diesel and/or an automatic transmission; special air cleaning systems for the engine are a virtual standard.

A front-mounted winch is another optional extra.

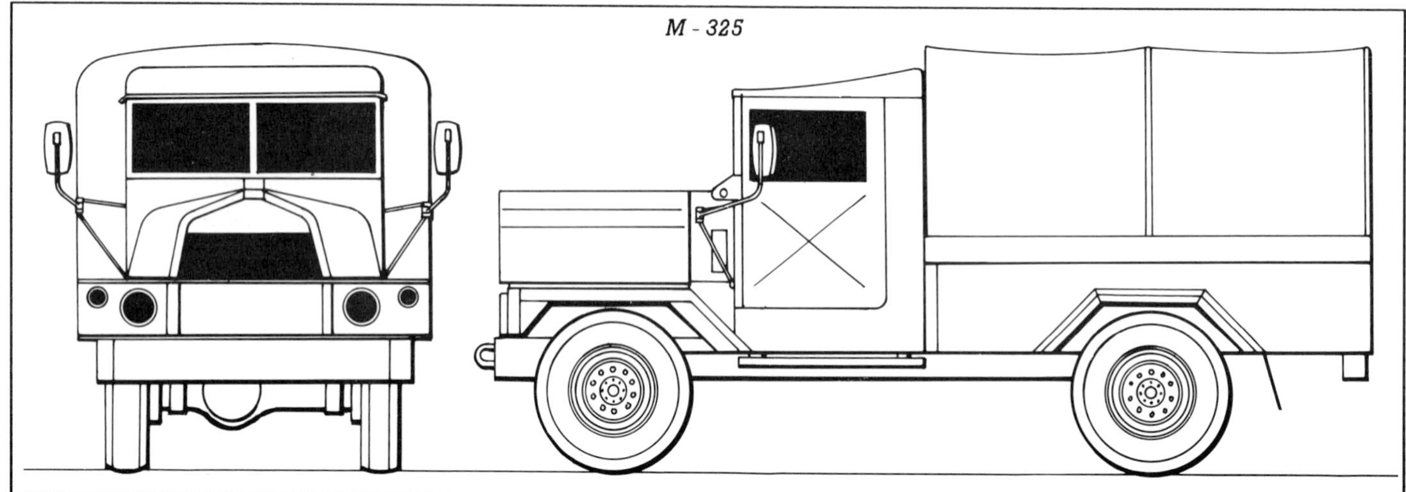

Specification

Role: light utility vehicle
Cab seating: 1 + 1
Configuration: 4 x 4
Weight: (empty) approx 2550 kg
Max load: 1950 kg
Length: 5.073 m
Width: 2.08 m
Height: 2.37 m
Ground clearance: 0.4 m
Track: 1.715 m
Wheelbase: 3.2 m
Max speed: (road) 100 km/h
Fuel capacity: 144 litres
Fording: 0.76 m
Engine: Chrysler OHC 225-2 LC 3.687 litre 6 cylinder petrol
Power output: 100 hp/3600 rpm
Gearbox: manual, 4f, 1r
Clutch: Borg & Beck single dry plate
Transfer box: NP-200-D 2-speed
Steering: worm and roller
Turning circle: 14.2 m
Suspension: leaf springs and shock absorbers
Tyres: 9.00 x 16-10 ply
Electrical system: 24 V

Variants: see text

M-325 Commandcar with roll bars and machine gun pintles

M-462 Abir

The **M-462 Abir** was developed by Automotive Industries using the considerable experience gained in producing the **M- 325 Commandcar** (see previous entry) and it is anticipated that many of the roles currently carried out by the M-325 will be assumed by the **Abir**. The **Abir** is a completely new design with a V8 diesel engine, an automatic transmission and a new chassis providing good ground clearance combined with a low centre of gravity. It was developed using resources from within Israel and with Israeli operational conditions (and economic operation over extended periods) in mind so it is a tough and versatile vehicle capable of sustained operations under adverse conditions.

The list of variants follows the same general lines as the M-325 (qv), including a general purpose cargo and personnel carrier, but there are a few roles special to the **Abir**. One is a completely open TOW (or the Israeli laser-guided version, the MAPATS) missile launcher anti-tank vehicle while another is an internal security vehicle with wire mesh shields for the windscreen, a clear plastic roof for the cab and rear area, and similar side screens to protect the passengers (up to 12) in the rear. A version with a shortened cargo area can be used as a mortar or light artillery tractor and there are both forward and rear area ambulance variants.

An armoured patrol version has been proposed and there is an internal security version armed with a pulsating water cannon. The **W-1000** is a forest fire fighting vehicle. Most versions of the **Abir** have a soft-topped cab and removable canvas doors but options include a hard-top cab (with air conditioning if required), metal doors, and a 4500 kg winch.

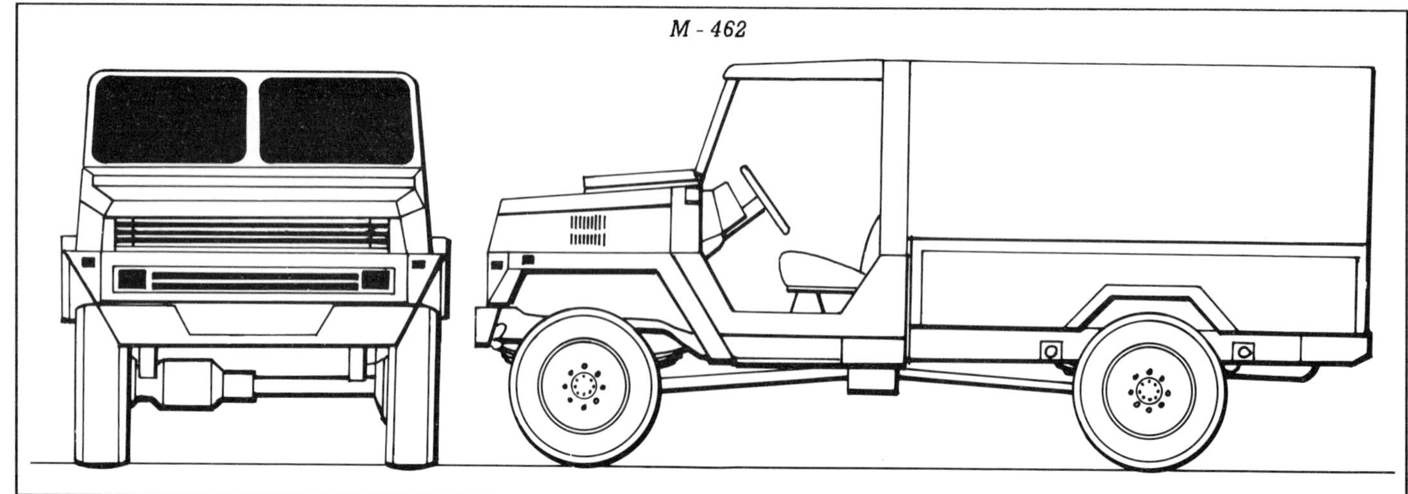

Specification

Role: light utility vehicle
Cab seating: 1 + 2
Configuration: 4 x 4
Weight: (empty) approx 2600 kg
Max load: 1890 kg
Length: 5.03 m
Width: 2.04 m
Height: 2.1 m
Ground clearance: 0.4 m
Track: 1.7 m
Wheelbase: 3 m
Max speed: (road) 115 km/h
Fuel capacity: 144 litres
Fording: 0.4 m
Engine: 6.2 litre V8 diesel
Power output: 145 hp/3600 rpm
Gearbox: automatic, 3f, 1r
Clutch: single dry plate
Transfer box: NP 205 2-speed
Steering: power assisted
Turning circle: 14.2 m
Suspension: leaf springs and shock absorbers
Tyres: 9.00 x 16-10 ply
Electrical system: 24 V

Variants: see text

M462 Abir multi-purpose tactical truck in police patrol/anti-riot form

IVECO 40-10 WM

Italy

The **IVECO 40-10 WM** is the result of a gradual development to produce a light utility military truck using the commercial **FIAT Daily** as a basis. One of the first stages in development was the air-portable **FIAT 40 PM** and further development resulted in the more versatile **40-10 WM**. The **40-10 WM** still shows its commercial origins visually but the original has been considerably strengthened and fully militarised to the point where it is now one of IVECO's main export successes of recent years.

Significant numbers have been sold to Pakistan and Belgium (for use by the Gendarmerie) and over 600 are in service with the Italian armed forces, especially with mountain warfare units. The type is in licence production in Canada for the military there.

The **40-10 WM** in its general utility form has the usual cargo area that can be converted to carry up to ten troops; the cargo area can also be used to accommodate a standard 1.5 tonne communications shelter. Box bodies can be used for command and ambulance versions while an open variant with a removable soft-topped cab may be used to carry either a 106 mm recoilless rifle or some form of anti-tank missile launcher.

More mundane variants include a field refuelling vehicle, mobile workshops, internal security and other police vehicles, and light fire or crash tenders.

The **40-10 WM** is powerful enough to tow light artillery pieces such as the OTO Melara 105 mm Pack Howitzer.

The **IVECO 40-10 WM** is also air portable as two can be carried inside a C-130 transport aircraft.

Optional equipment includes a winch and both right- and left-hand drive versions are available.

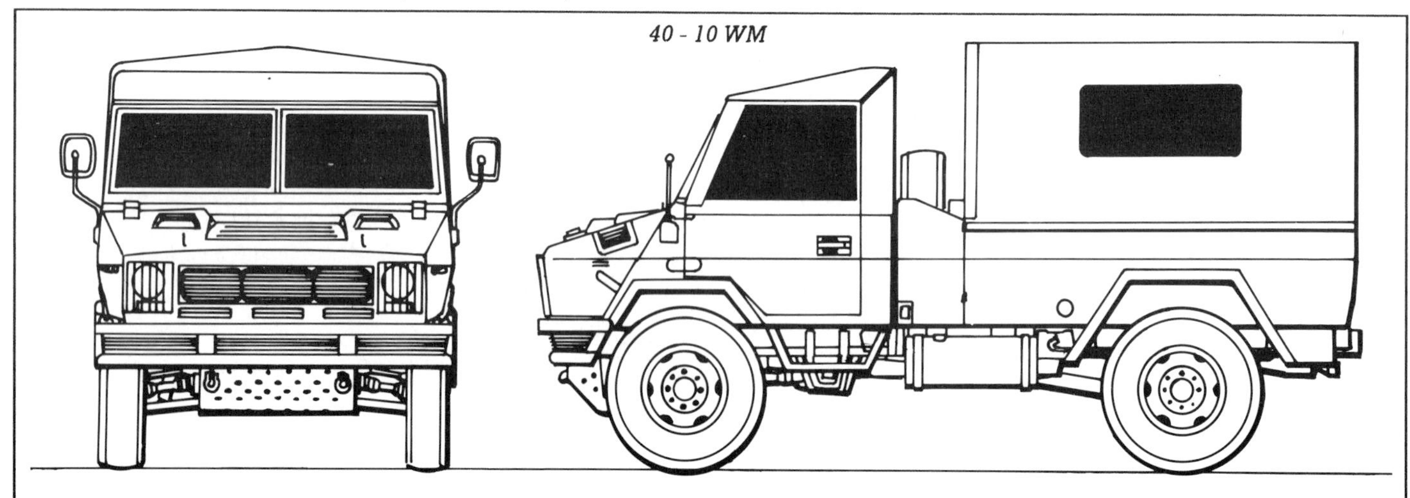

Specification

Role: light utility vehicle
Cab seating: 1 + 2
Configuration: 4 x 4
Weight: (empty) 2800 kg
Max load: 1500 kg
Length: 4.645 m
Width: 2 m
Height: 2.38 m
Ground clearance: 0.26 m
Track: 1.67 m
Wheelbase: 2.8 m
Max speed: (road) 100 km/h
Fuel capacity: 70 litres
Fording: 0.7 m
Engine: FIAT 8142 2.5 litre 4 cylinder turbocharged diesel
Power output: 103 hp/3800 rpm
Gearbox: manual, 5f, 1r
Clutch: single dry plate
Transfer box: 2-speed
Steering: hydraulic power assisted
Turning circle: 12 m
Suspension: front, independent torsion bars; rear leaf springs
Tyres: 9.00 R 16
Electrical system: 24 V

Variants: see text

IVECO 40-10 WM carrying fire fighting equipment

IVECO 90-17 WM

Italy

The **IVECO 90-17 WM** emerged during the mid-1970s as one of a family of FIAT trucks developed for both military and commercial sales and known as the 'Bolzano' range (after their factory of origin) .

There were three basic models in this range, the **FIAT 65P, 75P** and **90P**, and these three spawned numerous derivatives.

The model destined to be the 4 tonne class military general utility and load carrier became the **90-17 WM**, known to the Italian Army as the ACM-80 (*Autocarro Medio 1980*). Sharing many components with the lighter but generally similar **IVECO 75-14 WM** which was also used by the Italian armed forces.

The conventional design of the **IVECO 90-17 WM** features an all- steel forward control cab that can be tilted forward for maintenance, and an all-steel cargo area which may be converted to carry up to 18 troops on folding bench seats. Loads up to 4000 kg can be carried in the cargo area and a rear towing hook allows a further 4000 kg to be towed in a trailer.

Variants of the basic general utility truck include a light recovery vehicle, various mobile workshops, a tanker for fuel or water, and a fire- fighting vehicle.

The **IVECO 90-17 WM** can also be used as a light artillery tractor.

Optional equipment includes a winch mounted at the front or rear, a lockable front differential, and larger tyres.

It appears that the **IVECO 90-17 WM** is used only by the Italian armed forces and Somalia.

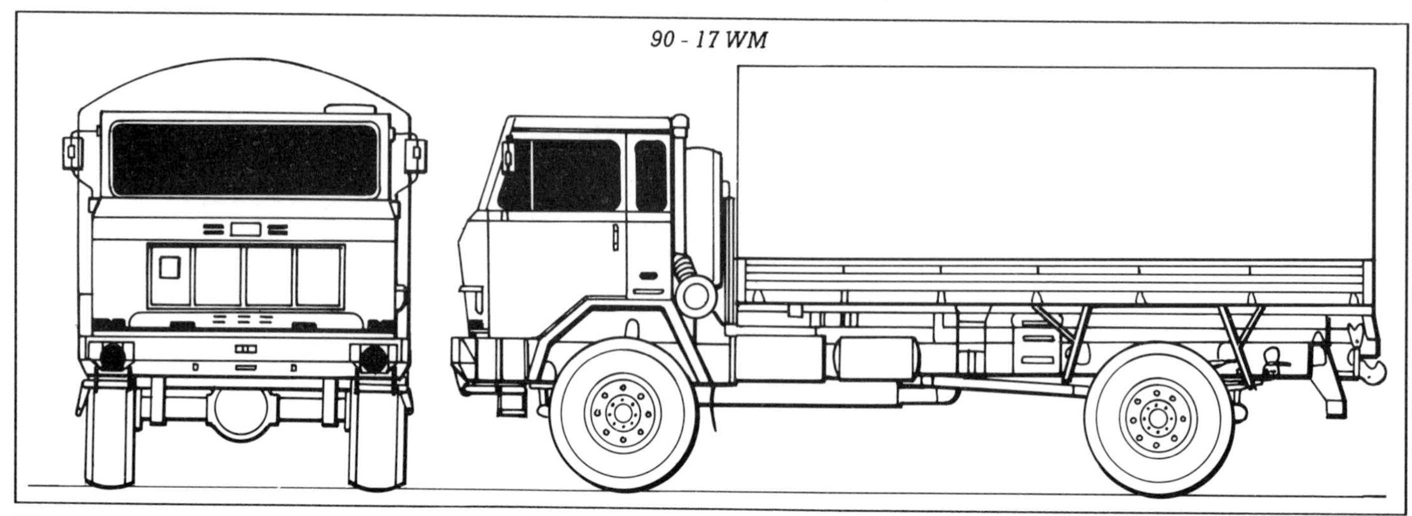

Specification

Role: general utility truck
Cab seating: 1 + 1
Configuration: 4 x 4
Weight: (empty) 5740 kg
Max load: 4000 kg
Length: 6.358 m
Width: 2.3 m
Height: 2.96 m
Ground clearance: 0.445 m
Track: 1.852 m
Wheelbase: 3.7 m
Max speed: (road) over 80 km/h
Fuel capacity: 155 litres
Fording: 0.7 m
Engine: FIAT Model 8060.25 5.86 litre 6 cylinder supercharged diesel
Power output: 170 hp/3000 rpm
Gearbox: manual, 5f, 1r
Clutch: single dry plate
Transfer box: 2-speed
Steering: recirculating ball
Turning circle: 15 m
Suspension: leaf springs with shock absorbers
Tyres: 12.5 R 20 PR
Electrical system: 24 V

Variants: see text

IVECO 90.17 WM 4 tonne general purpose truck

IVECO 230-35 WM

Italy

The **IVECO 230-35 WM** is the artillery truck/tractor version of a series of vehicles that includes general purpose trucks and a recovery vehicle. The vehicle is a development of the earlier **FIAT 230 PM 26** and **230 PM 35**, which were essentially similar vehicles using differing engines and transmissions; neither remains in production.

The **IVECO 230-35 WM** is orthodox in design, having an all-steel forward control cab which is usually fitted with a soft top; a hard top with an observation hatch is optional. The all-steel cargo area is fitted with the usual removable drop sides and tailgate and is normally covered by a canvas tilt over bows. Folding bench seats for up to 22 troops are provided along each side of the cargo area but when used as an artillery tractor the cargo body is divided into two halves. One half, which may be removed when required, is accommodation for a gun crew of up to ten men while the other half is provided with ammunition racks and space for other associated supplies.

Other specialised equipment can include an ammunition pallet handling crane and a rear-mounted jib for lifting artillery trail legs on and off the towing hook. The artillery tractor can tow weapons weighing up to 15,000 kg.

Other suggested roles for the **230-35 WM** include mobile workshops, acting as a carrier for a flatrack load handling system, a fuel or water tanker, and various van bodies that could include a mobile medical post.

It has also been proposed that the **230-35 WM** could be used as a carrier or support vehicle for missile or other weapon systems.

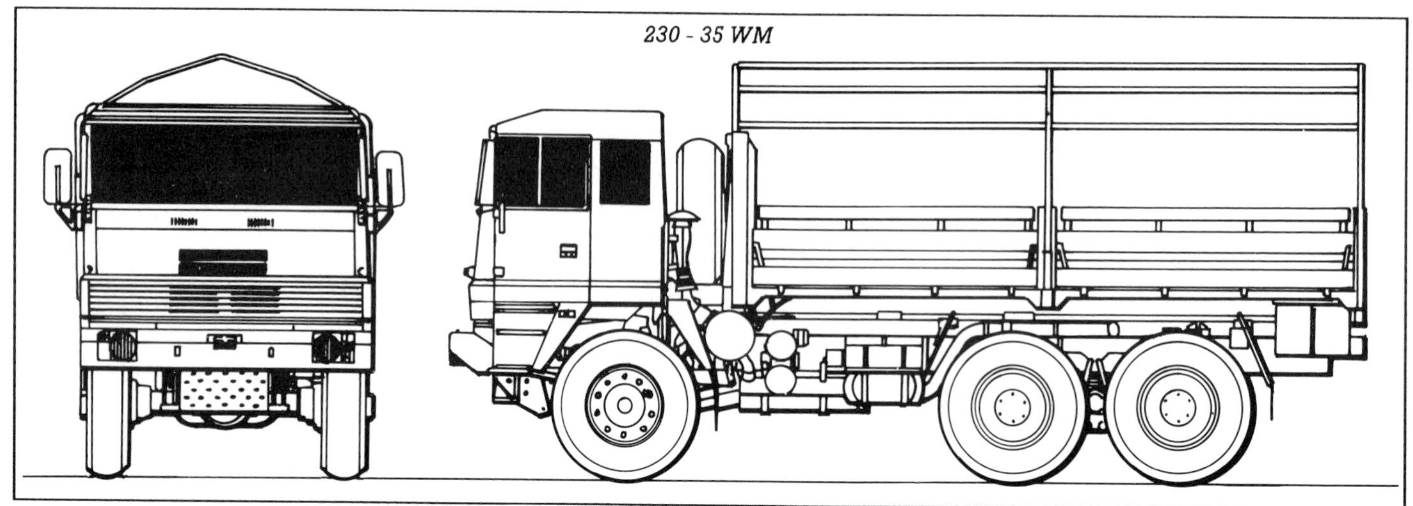
230 - 35 WM

Specification

Role: general utility truck and artillery tractor
Cab seating: 1 + 2
Configuration: 6 x 6
Weight: (empty) 13,000 kg
Max load: 10,000 kg
Length: 7.762 m
Width: 2.5 m
Height: 3.43 m
Ground clearance: 0.36 m

Track: 2.027 m/2.032 m
Wheelbase: 3.3 m + 1.38 m
Max speed: (road) over 80 km/h
Fuel capacity: 300 litres
Fording: 1.2 m
Engine: FIAT 8280.02 17.174 litre V8 diesel
Power output: 352 hp/2400 rpm
Gearbox: ZF 4 S 150 GPA with torque converter, 8f, 1r

Clutch: none - torque converter
Transfer box: lockable
Steering: recirculating ball, power assisted
Turning circle: 19 m
Suspension: leaf springs and shock absorbers
Tyres: 14.00 x 20
Electrical system: 24 V

Variants: see text

IVECO 230-35 WM 6 x 6 artillery truck-tractor towing 155 mm FH-70 howitzer

Type 73 4 x 4 Japan

As it's designation implies, the **Type 73** 4 x 4 truck was standardised for service with the Japanese Ground Self- Defence Force in 1973 as a measure to replace the numerous types of light and medium utility trucks then in service.

The **Type 73** is a fully militarised version of the **Toyota WB500** light truck manufactured by Hino Motors, a Toyota Motor Company associate, so the vehicle is sometimes known as the **Hino WB500**. The **Type 73** 4 x 4 has a seemingly oversized over-engine cab with internal space for the driver, one passenger and their personal equipment. Normally provided with a soft top and a forward-folding windscreen, the cab is provided with a heater-defrost system for use in less temperate areas.

The all-steel cargo area can be covered by the usual heavy canvas tilt and has a typical Japanese military feature in that wooden side stakes and rails can be folded down to act as personnel benches. The tail-gate has an integral folding step to assist personnel mounting the cargo area.

The **Type 73** can be used to carry mortars and their crews. Only one variant of the **Type 73** is known to have been formalised and that is a fully-enclosed van-bodied ambulance, but forward area ambulances with stretcher racks in the cargo area have been seen.

Some vehicles are equipped with a hot weather cooling system and a front-mounted winch may also be fitted.

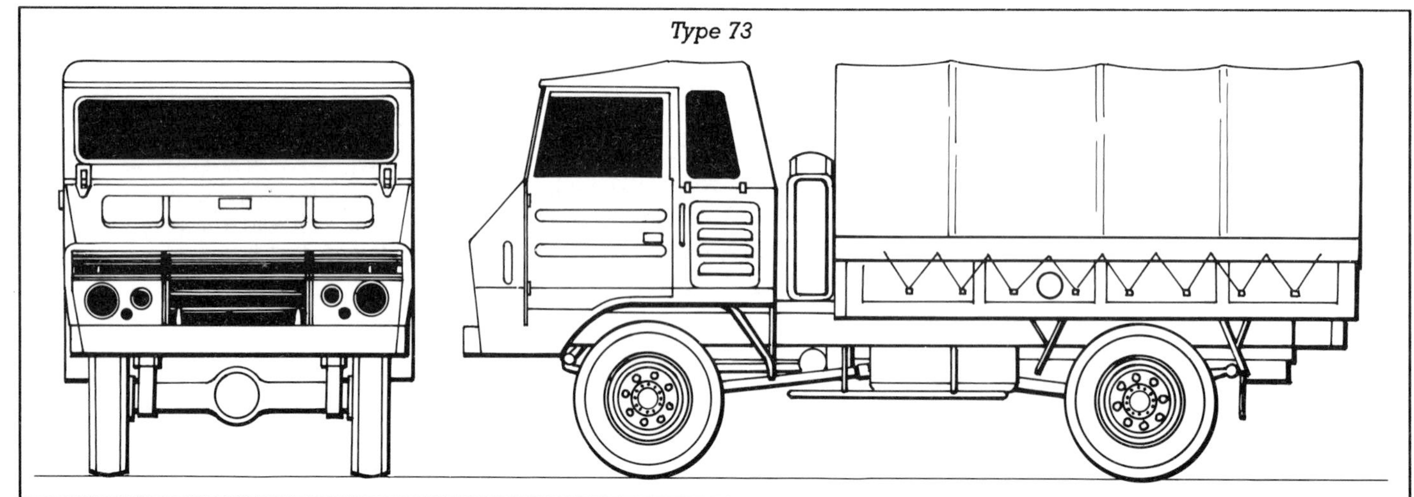
Type 73

Specification

Role: light utility truck
Cab seating: 1 + 1
Configuration: 4 x 4
Weight: (empty) 3195 kg
Max load: (on road) 2000 kg
Length: 5.36 m
Width: 2.09 m
Height: 2.49 m
Ground clearance: 0.28 m
Track: 1.61 m/1.635 m
Wheelbase: 2.9 m
Max speed: (road) 87 km/h
Fuel capacity: 115 litres
Fording: 0.8 m
Engine: Hino DQ100 4.3 litre 6 cylinder diesel
Power output: 95 hp/3000 rpm
Gearbox: manual, 5f, 1r
Clutch: single dry plate
Transfer box: 2-speed
Steering: recirculating ball
Turning circle: 12.8 m
Suspension: leaf springs with shock absorbers
Tyres: 8.25 x 20
Electrical system: 24 V

Variants: see text

Japanese Self-Defence Forces Type 73 4 x 4 2 tonne truck

DAF YA 4442 DNT

Netherlands

The **DAF YA 4442 DNT** is visually similar to the earlier **YA 4440**, the first of the latter being delivered to the Netherlands Army during 1976; the **YA 4440** was also licence-produced in Portugal. In its turn the **YA 4440** was based on experience gained with the **DAF YA 2442**, a commercial 4 x 2 design that did not enter production. The first **YA 4442 DNT** entered production during 1988 and it is anticipated that the final production total will be over 12,000 units.

The **YA 4442 DNT** uses many well-proven commercial components and differs from the earlier **YA 4440** in the installation of a new DAF DNT series turbocharged diesel engine, a new radiator grill and changes to the cab; there are also modifications to the brake and electrical systems. In design terms the **YA 4442 DNT** is entirely orthodox and has a forward control, forward tilting all-steel cab with a roof hatch combined with an optional machine gun ring mounting. The all-steel cargo area can be covered by the usual canvas tilt and seating provision is made for up to 18 troops. Single or dual tyres can be fitted to the rear wheels. If required the side boards and tail gate can be removed to allow the vehicle to carry shelters or containers.

There are three main variants. The **YA 4442 DNT** is the base general purpose cargo version; the **YAL 4442 DNT** is similar but has an enlarged cab for driver training with seating for the trainee driver, an instructor and two observer trainees; the **YAK 4442 DNT** is a cargo vehicle with a hydraulic loading crane plus stabiliser legs which are lowered when the crane is in operation.

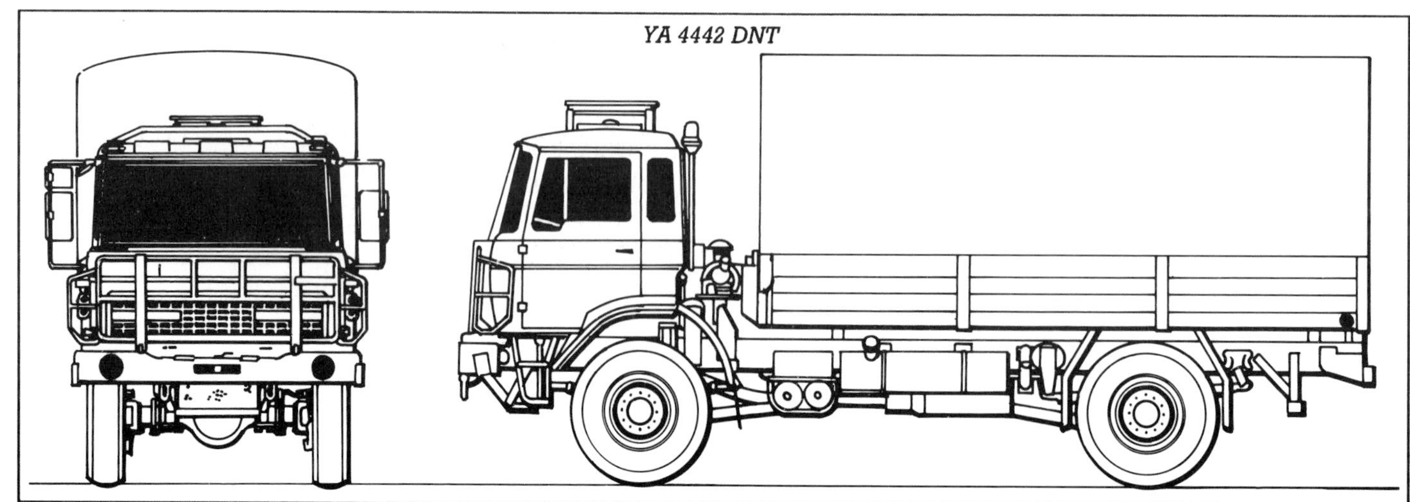
YA 4442 DNT

Specification

Role: general utility truck
Cab seating: 1 + 1
Configuration: 4 x 4
Weight: (empty) 7620 kg
Max load: 4000 kg
Length: 7.3 m
Width: 2.47 m
Height: 3.42 m
Ground clearance: 0.29 m
Track: 1.9 m/1.8 m
Wheelbase: 4.05 m
Max speed: (road) 93 km/h
Fuel capacity: 200 litres
Fording: 0.9 m
Engine: DAF DNT 620 6.242 litre 6 cylinder turbocharged diesel
Power output: 172 hp/2600 rpm
Gearbox: ZF S6-36 manual, 6f, 1r
Clutch: single dry plate
Transfer box: Steyr VG 450 2-speed
Steering: ZF 8043 power assisted
Turning circle: approx 19.6 m
Suspension: leaf springs and shock absorbers
Tyres: 13 R 22.5
Electrical system: 24 V

Variants: YA 4440, YA 4442 DNT, YAL 4442 DNT, YAK 4442 DNT

DAF YA 4442 DNT 4 x 4 4 tonne truck

DAF YAV 2300 DHTD

Netherlands

The **DAF YAV 2300 DHTD** is an early 1980's 4 x 4 development of the **DAF YAZ 2300** 6 x 6 truck (see following entry) and is described as a new generation military general purpose truck based on the extensive use of proven components selected from DAF's commercial vehicle range.

The **YAV 2300 DHTD** uses the same all-steel cab (a derivative of the DAF F 218) as the **YAZ 2300**, and dual tyres are fitted to the two rear wheels.

Overall the design is completely orthodox so the rear area is covered by a tilt and the drop sides and tail gate can be removed to allow the resultant flat bed to carry various forms of shelter or ISO containers.

The payload on roads is up to 8000 kg; across country it is limited to 5300 kg. The flatbed has been used to carry a DAF fuel field distribution unit.

Other loads carried by the **YAZ 2300 DHTD** include a Dornier telescopic aerial mast.

Numbers of these trucks are in service with various NATO field headquarters as prime movers for the associated shelters and electronic equipment. Some of the vehicles involved are **YTV 2300** tractor trucks for towing semi-trailers weighing up to 20,000 kg, including fuel and water tanker semi-trailers.

Engine and other modifications can be introduced to the **YAV 2300 DHTD** to allow operations under extremes of climate.

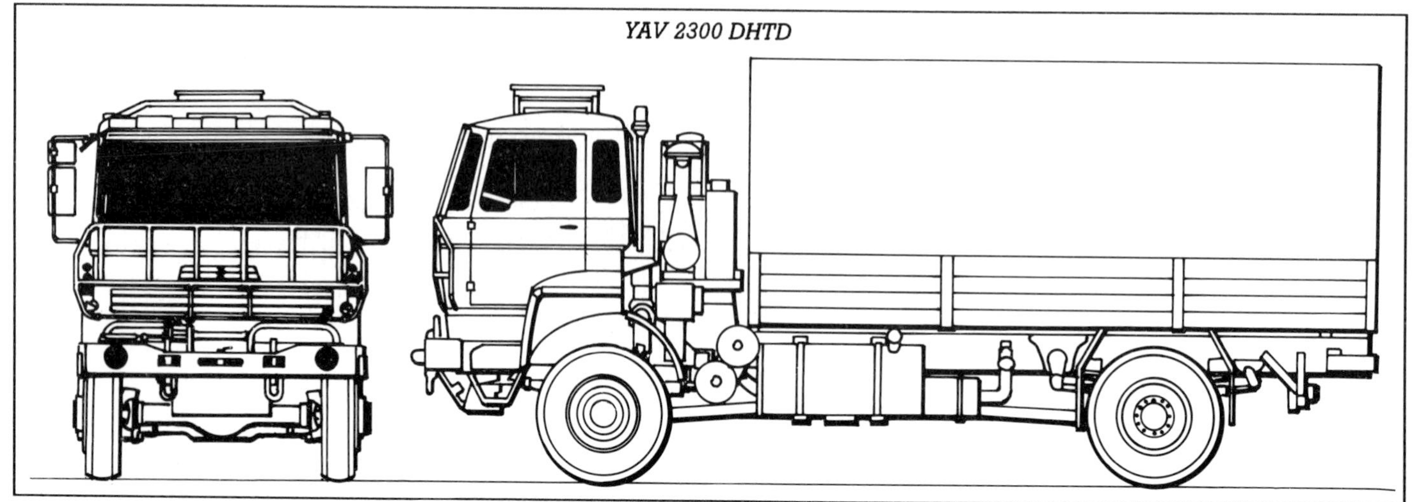
YAV 2300 DHTD

Specification

Role: general utility truck
Cab seating: 1 + 1 or 2
Configuration: 4 x 4
Weight: (empty) 10,200 kg
Max load: 5300 kg
Length: 7.82 m
Width: 2.46 m
Height: (cab) 3.1 m
Ground clearance: 0.32 m
Track: 1.98 m/1.82 m
Wheelbase: 4.5 m
Max speed: (road) 88 km/h
Fuel capacity: 300 litres
Fording: 0.9 m
Engine: DAF DHTD 825 Mil 8.25 litre 6 cylinder turbocharged diesel
Power output: 213 hp/2400 rpm
Gearbox: ZF 56 111 GPA, 8f, 1r
Clutch: none - torque converter
Transfer box: ZF A 600/30 2-speed
Steering: ZF 8046 power assisted
Turning circle: (minimum) 18 m
Suspension: leaf springs and shock absorbers
Tyres: 13 R 22.5K or 14.75/80 R 20
Electrical system: 24 V

Variants: YAV 2300 DHTD, YTV 2300

DAF YAV 2300 DHTD 4 x 4 truck carrying fuel transfer equipment

DAF YAZ 2300 DHS

The **DAF YAZ 2300** 6 x 6 truck series was ordered into production for the Netherlands armed forces during 1981 to replace older DAF trucks and was described at the time as the product of a new generation of military truck design. The **YAZ 2300** series was based on the **DAF 2300** series of commercial trucks but was extensively militarised and the DHS 825 turbocharged diesel was installed at the front end of a strong ladder chassis frame.

The **YAZ 2300 DHS** is a 10 tonne general purpose truck fitted with a modified DAF F 218 cab which carries over civilian standards in sound and thermal insulation and adjustable seats; a larger four-man cab is also available.

A hydraulic materials handling crane may be fitted behind the cab while the cargo area is surrounded on both sides by removable three-section drop side panels; there is also a tail gate.

Variants of the base cargo model include the **YKZ 2300**, a three-way tipper truck, and the **YGZ 2300** bridging vehicle used to carry and launch/recover Ribbon Bridge sections or bridge erection boats.

The **YHZ 2300** is a special artillery tractor version only 7.74 metres long which is used to tow 155 mm M114 or M114/39 howitzers; it carries a crew of up to nine gunners and 24 rounds of ready-use ammunition.

Two special variants are used to support the Patriot tactical air defence missile system - the **YAZ 2301** is used to carry control equipment shelters while the **YTZ 2301** is a tractor truck used to tow the missile launcher.

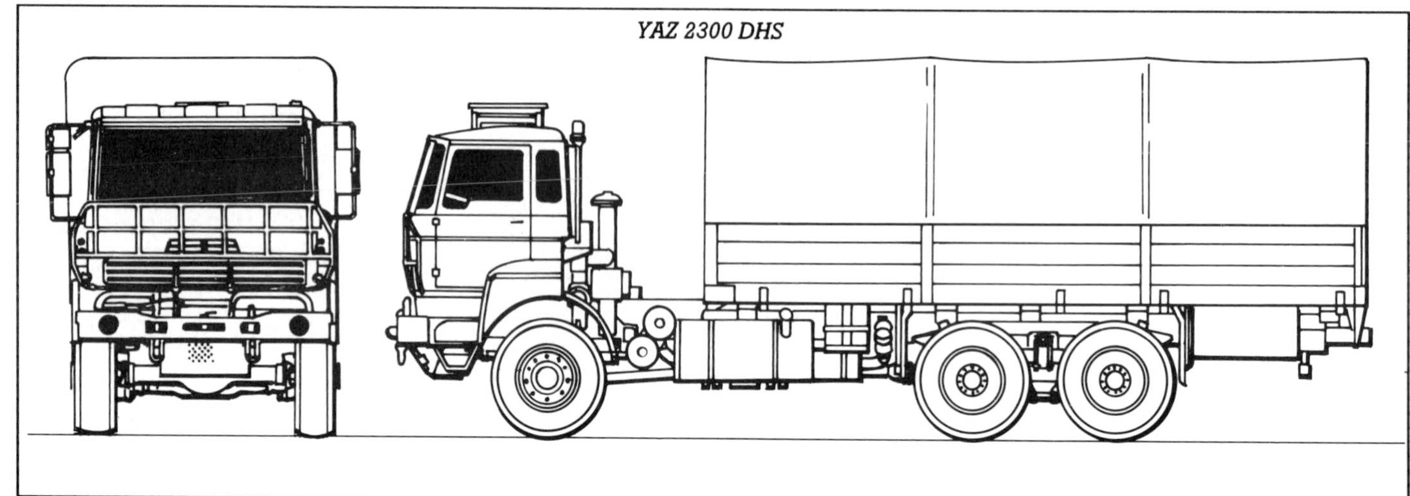

YAZ 2300 DHS

Specification

Role: general utility truck
Cab seating: 1 + 1 or 2
Configuration: 6 x 6
Weight: (empty) 11,600 kg
Max load: 10,000 kg
Length: 9.55 m
Width: 2.49 m
Height: (cab) 3.02 m
Ground clearance: 0.32 m
Track: 1.98 m/1.82 m
Wheelbase: 4.45 m
Max speed: (road) 88 km/h
Fuel capacity: 300 litres
Fording: 0.75 m
Engine: DAF DHS 825 8.25 litre 6 cylinder turbocharged diesel
Power output: 250 hp/2400 rpm
Gearbox: ZF 5 S-111 GPA, 8f, 1r
Clutch: none, torque converter
Transfer box: ZF A 600/3D 2-speed
Steering: ZF 8046 power assisted
Turning circle: 22.4 m
Suspension: leaf springs and shock absorbers
Tyres: 13 R 22.5
Electrical system: 24 V

Variants: YAZ 2300 DHS, YKZ 2300, YGZ 2300, YHZ 2300, YAZ 2301, YTZ 2301

DAF YHZ 2300 DHS, the artillery tractor component of the DAF YAZ 2300 10 tonne 6 x 6 truck range

When the United Nations placed an embargo on defence material exports to South Africa the South Africans were forced to use their own resources to provide themselves with equipment and armaments. They formed South African Military (SAMIL) to manufacture military trucks, one of which became the 2-tonne light utility vehicle, the **SAMIL 20**. Based on the Unimog chassis design, but with many locally-incorporated features, the **SAMIL 20** became the base component of a large range of vehicles but the cargo vehicle has been produced in the largest numbers. This has a soft-topped forward control cab and a high cargo bed able to seat up to ten soldiers, but the main feature of the **SAMIL 20** is its extreme toughness, provided to enable the vehicle to survive under harsh South African conditions.

Numerous variants have been produced, one being a cargo vehicle with an armoured mine-proof cab to protect the occupants against land mine explosions - this cab can be fitted to other **SAMIL 20** variants. Other armoured variants include the open **Bulldog** (the similar **Buffel** uses a Unimog chassis) and the fully enclosed **Rhino**, both armoured personnel carriers. The **SAMIL 20** is also used as the launch vehicle for the Valkiri 1 22 127 mm artillery rocket system.

Van-bodied vehicles are used for everything from artillery fire control vehicles to ambulances and mobile workshops. The cargo area can also be used to carry containers and shelters. The **SAMIL 20** has been replaced in production by the **SAMIL 20 Mark 2** which is powered by an Atlantis Diesel Engine (ADE) 352N and which incorporates more components of local origin.

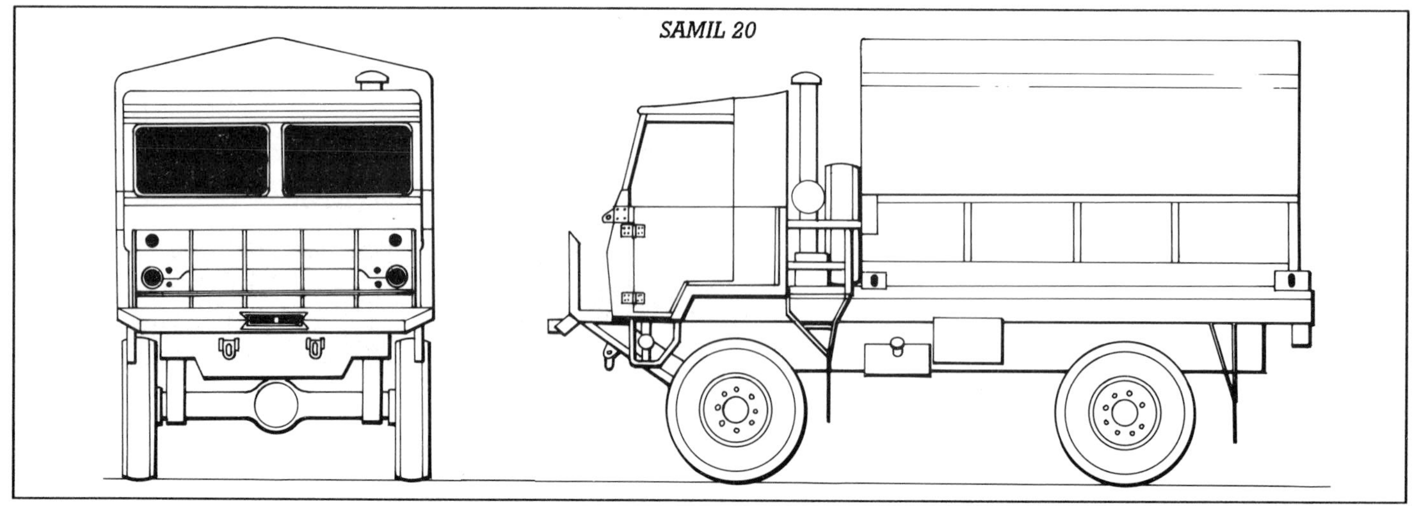

SAMIL 20

Specification

Role: light utility truck
Cab seating: 1 + 1
Configuration: 4 x 4
Weight: (empty) 4580 kg
Max load: 2000 kg
Length: 5.692 m
Width: 2.438 m
Height: 2.82 m
Ground clearance: 0.47 m
Track: 1.852 m
Wheelbase: 2.9 m
Max speed: (road) 90 km/h
Fuel capacity: 200 litres
Fording: 1.2 m
Engine: 6.128 litre 6 cylinder diesel
Power output: 104 hp/2650 rpm
Gearbox: manual, 5f, 1r
Clutch: single dry plate
Transfer box: 2-speed
Steering: ball and nut, power assisted
Turning circle: 12 m
Suspension: leaf springs and shock absorbers
Tyres: 14.5 x 20 PR 12
Electrical system: 24 V

Variants: Bulldog, Rhino

SAMIL 20 4 x 4 2-tonne truck with general purpose body

SAMIL 50

South Africa

The **SAMIL 50** was based on the design of the **Magirus-Deutz 192D12A1**(now the **IVECO Magirus 120-19 ANWM** - qv) but was considerably modified locally to make thė vehicle considerably stronger and incorporate locally-available components. The **SAMIL 50** is now one of the standard South African Defence Forces vehicles and is used in large numbers. Visually it resembles the Magirus Deutz original but there are many detail changes and the **SAMIL 50** is able to remain operational for extended periods even under the harshest South African operational conditions.

The **SAMIL 50** is used as the basis for an extended range of vehicles, all of which can be fitted with an armoured mine-proof cab. Removable bench seats in the rear can carry up to 40 troops and a virtual permanent fixture used in operational areas is a twin-axle trailer carrying up to 6000 kg.

Variants include a recovery vehicle, fuel and water tankers, and a series of box-bodied vehicles which include various types of mobile workshop and a mobile refrigerated pantry. There is also a mobile battery-charging vehicle. Telecommunication shelters may be carried on the cargo bed. An armoured mine-protected ambulance was produced at one time but has been discontinued. The original **SAMIL 50** has now been replaced in production by the **SAMIL 50 Mark 2** which has an enlarged bonnet to accommodate a new ADE 409N 9.5 litre 5 cylinder diesel engine.

The Mark 2 incorporates more components of local origin, including a strengthened front axle. A 7 tonne 4 x 2 version, the **SAKOM 50**, uses a SAMIL 20 cab and is employed on second-line duties.

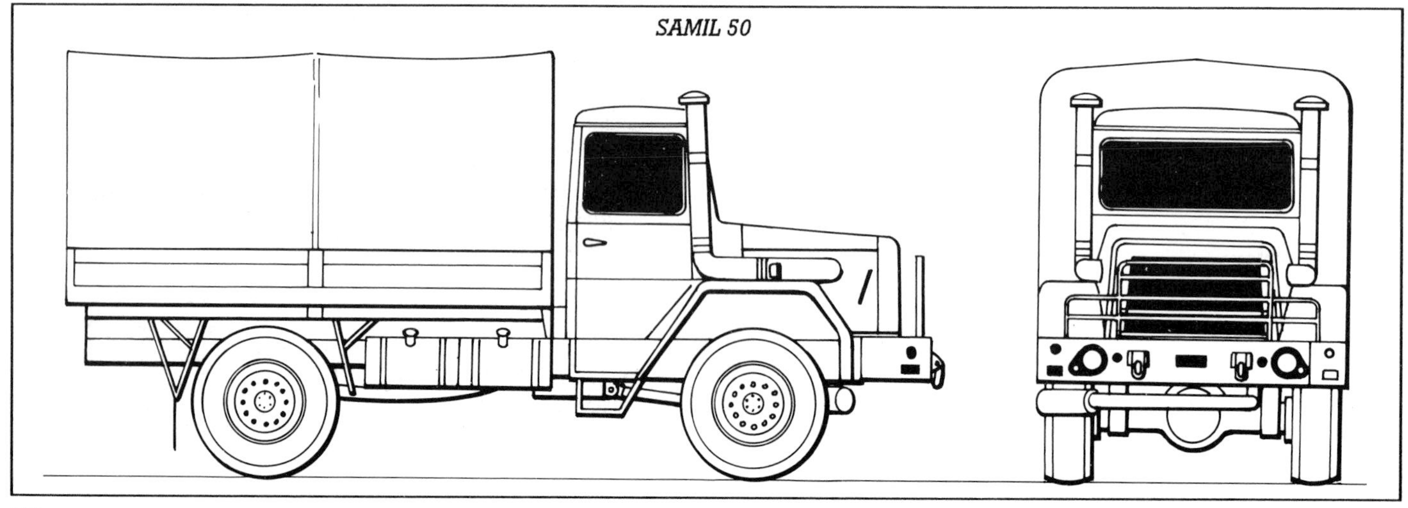
SAMIL 50

Specification

Role: general utility truck
Cab seating: 1 + 2
Configuration: 4 x 4
Weight: (empty) 6255 kg
Max load: 4800 kg
Length: 7.78 m
Width: 2.45 m
Height: 2.95 m
Ground clearance: 0.355 m
Track: 2.03 m
Wheelbase: 4.9 m
Max speed: (road) 90 km/h
Fuel capacity: 400 litres
Fording: 1.2 m
Engine: 9.57 litre V6 diesel
Power output: 157 hp/2650 rpm
Gearbox: manual, 6f, 1r
Clutch: single dry plate
Transfer box: 2-speed
Steering: ball and nut, power assisted
Turning circle: 23 m
Suspension: leaf springs and shock absorbers
Tyres: 14.00 x 20 PR 18
Electrical system: 24 V

Variants: see text

SAMIL 50 4 x 4 truck with workshop body

SAMIL 100

The **SAMIL 100** is virtually a SAMIL 50 (qv) with an extra axle at the rear and a more powerful V-10 diesel engine. It shares many components (such as the cab) with the SAMIL 50 and is again based on Magirus-Deutz models, although considerably strengthened to suit local conditions and incorporating many locally-available components.

The **SAMIL 100** is the standard heavy load-carrying vehicle of the South African Defence Forces and is used in many versions, apart from the basic cargo drop-sided model. Some of the cargo models are fitted with material handling cranes. There is a heavy recovery vehicle in the **SAMIL 100** range, plus a heavy tipper truck, water and fuel tankers, and a specialised artillery tractor used to tow and support the 155 mm G-5 gun-howitzer. The artillery tractor carries a crew cabin and a hydraulic ammunition-handling crane. Food-orientated variants include a mobile canteen, a panel-bodied truck used to carry perishable products and what must be one of the most unusual of all military truck roles, a mobile beer cooler. Another unusual variant is a horse transporter with a mine-protected cab and more armour extending the whole length of the underside. Most of the other variants can be fitted with an armoured mine-proof cab. A 6 x 4 variant for use in rear areas has been produced; some are used by commercial and police organisations.

As with the other SAMIL trucks, a **SAMIL 100 Mark 2** is now in production. This has a locally-produced V10 diesel engine and some other components of South African origin.

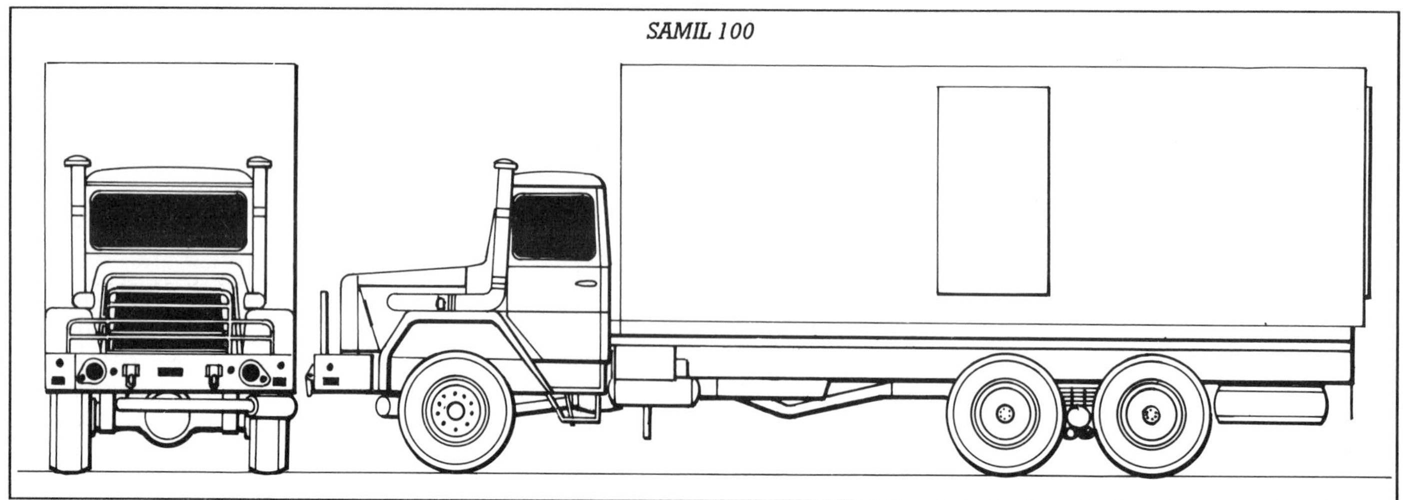

SAMIL 100

Specification

Role: heavy utility truck and artillery tractor
Cab seating: 1 + 2
Configuration: 6 x 6
Weight: (empty) 9135 kg
Max load: 10,000 kg
Length: 10.27 m
Width: 2.5 m
Height: 3.35 m
Ground clearance: 0.35 m
Track: 2.002 m/2.048 m
Wheelbase: 5.25 m + 1.38 m
Max speed: (road) 90 km/h
Fuel capacity: 400 litres
Fording: 1.2 m
Engine: V10 air-cooled diesel
Power output: 268 hp/2650 rpm
Gearbox: manual, 6f, 1r
Clutch: single dry plate
Transfer box: 2-speed
Steering: ball and nut, power assisted
Turning circle: 23.8 m
Suspension: leaf springs and shock absorbers
Tyres: 14.00 x 20 PR 18
Electrical system: 24 V

Variants: see text

SAMIL 100 6 x 6 truck with tanker body

GAZ - 66

The **GAZ-66** entered production during 1964 at the Gor'kiy Automobile Plant, where it replaced the earlier **GAZ- 63** on the lines. Originally produced for both civilian and military use, the military versions gradually became paramount and the **GAZ-66** is understood to be still in production. It has been produced in terms of hundreds of thousands and the overall design follows the usual Soviet guidelines of relative simplicity, strength and versatility. There are no design frills on the **GAZ-66** as it is an orthodox forward control design capable of being produced in, or modified into, many different versions.

The basic cargo/utility model has an all-steel cargo body with an optional canvas cover over bows mounted on a chassis frame that can be arranged to carry any number of body styles. Standard equipment includes a powerful cab heater and an engine pre-heater but these are omitted on models intended for tropical use. Models produced from 1968 onwards, the **GAZ-66A**, have a central tyre pressure regulation system and may feature a soft-top cab.

The **GAZ-66B** is modified for use by airborne forces. However there are numerous sub-variants, with or without winches, and with many equipped for special roles such as NBC decontamination, oil supply vehicles and numerous van-bodied versions for uses varying from command vehicles to mobile offices and communications centres. The **GAZ-66** is used to carry the 82 mm Vasilyek automatic mortar, a vehicle/weapon combination known as the 2B9. The **GAZ-66** is used by Warsaw Pact armed forces and wherever Soviet influence has spread. Many are used throughout the Middle East and nations in Africa such as Angola.

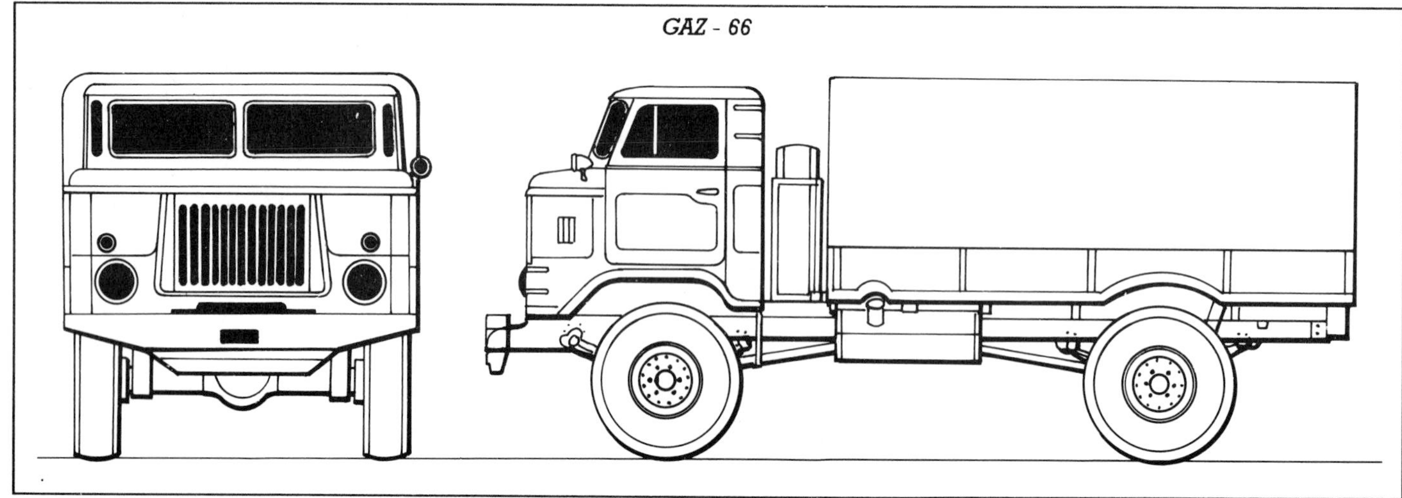
GAZ - 66

Specification

Role: light utility truck
Cab seating: 1 + 1
Configuration: 4 x 4
Weight: (empty) 3440 kg
Max load: 2000 kg
Length: 5.655 m
Width: 2.342 m
Height: 2.44 m
Ground clearance: 0.315 m
Track: 1.8 m/1.75 m
Wheelbase: 3.3 m
Max speed: (road) 95 km/h
Fuel capacity: 210 litres
Fording: 0.8 m
Engine: ZMZ 4.254 litre V 8 petrol
Power output: 115 hp/3200 rpm
Gearbox: manual, 4f, 1r
Clutch: single dry plate
Transfer box: 2-speed
Steering: worm and roller with hydraulic booster
Turning circle: 20 m
Suspension: leaf springs and shock absorbers
Tyres: 12.00 x 18
Electrical system: 12 V

Variants: GAZ-66, GAZ-66A, GAZ-66B

GAZ-66 4 x 4 truck with workshop body

Ural-375 and Ural-4320 Former Soviet Union

The **Ural 375** entered production in 1961. Powered by a 7 litre petrol engine, the main production model was the **Ural- 375D,** which was used as the basis for a wide range of body styles, but most were produced as standard 4 tonne cargo trucks; the **Ural-375T** was fitted with a winch while the **Ural- 377** series were 6 x 4 vehicles (including the **Ural-377S** truck tractor).

Many **Ural 375s** remain in service in many forms within former Warsaw Pact armed forces and elsewhere. They vary from multiple rocket launcher carriers to missile resupply vehicles and fuel servicing trucks

The specialised **TMS-65** is a special NBC decontamination vehicle carrying a jet engine to remove NBC agents from other vehicles. In 1973 a **Ural-375D** was fitted with a V 8 diesel engine and from 1978 onwards all production versions from the Ural Motor Vehicle Plant at Miass were fitted with the new engine.

Other production changes such as an enlarged bonnet plus revised fuel, cooling and electrical systems were introduced at the same time along with many other detail modifications. The designation became the **Ural-4320** under a new truck designation system and production continues.

It is anticipated that the **Ural-4320** will gradually take over many of the roles now carried out by the Ural-375 series.

Several **Ural-4320** production versions exist, mainly differing in details such as tyre sizes and the incorporation of a tyre pressure regulation system; the **Ural-4420** is a tractor truck. A recovery vehicle version is also produced.

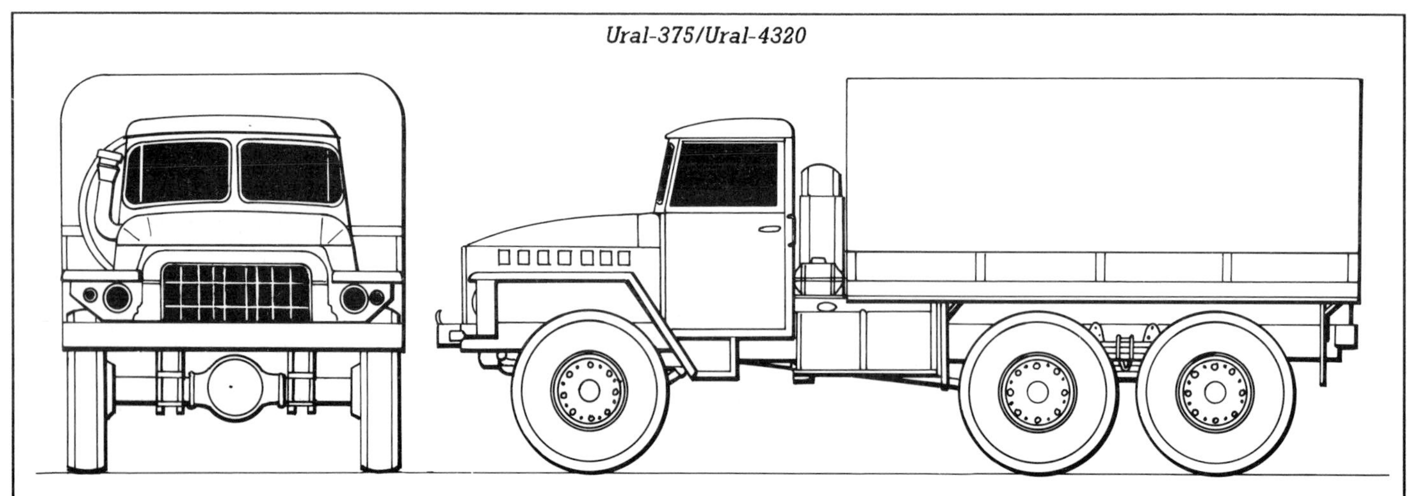

Ural-375/Ural-4320

Specification

Specification for Ural 4320

Role: general utility truck
Cab seating: 1 + 2
Configuration: 6 x 6
Weight: (empty) 8020 kg
Max load: 4500 kg
Length: 7.366 m
Width: 2.5 m
Height: 2.87 m
Ground clearance: 0.4 m
Track: 2 m
Wheelbase: 3.525 m + 1.4 m
Max speed: (road) 85 km/h
Fuel capacity: 210 + 60 litres
Fording: 1 m
Engine: KamAZ-740 10.85 litre V 8 diesel
Power output: 210 hp/2600 rpm
Gearbox: manual, 5f, 1r
Clutch: single dry plate
Transfer box: 2-speed
Steering: worm and gear
Turning circle: 22.8 m
Suspension: leaf springs and shock absorbers, check springs at rear
Tyres: 14.00 x 20
Electrical system: 24 V

Variants: Ural-375D, Ural-375T, Ural-377, Ural-377S, Ural-4320, Ural-4420, TMS-65

Ural-375 6 x 6 4-tonne truck

KamAZ-5320 Series

The **KamAZ-5320** series of trucks were introduced during 1976 and since then have become the work horses of the Soviet Union with the military and with civilian concerns. It is intended that in time they will replace many in-service vehicles with similar payloads. They are produced at the Kama Motor Vehicle Plant at Naberezhynye Chelmy (formerly Brezhnev) and there are numerous versions, both military and civil. The main military variant is the **KamAZ-4310**, introduced during 1982, which has a 6 x 6 drive configuration and a load capacity limited to 6000 kg across country; it also has a central tyre regulation system and can tow loads of up to 7000 kg. However the Soviet armed forces also make extensive use of many 6 x 4 models for many roles, including long-haul logistic supply. Most variants use the same forward control all-steel cab but body styles can vary to a great extent.

The basic **KamAZ-5320** is an 8 tonne cargo truck with an all-steel cargo body with down-folding sides and tailgate, all covered by a conventional canvas tilt over bows. The **KamAZ-5410** is a tractor truck while the **KamAZ-55102** is a tipper truck. Axle ratings can vary as can the type of engine fitted; the YaMZ-741 is a 260 hp V10 diesel while the YaMZ-7401 is a 180 hp V8. The standard naturally-aspirated YaMZ-740 V8 diesel engine is also used by the Ural- 4320 truck (qv) and some passenger buses. Some models have been fitted with German KHD 413 diesels but the numbers involved are believed to be relatively small.

Civil versions can have sleeper cabs and wheelbases can vary by an additional 0.5 m.

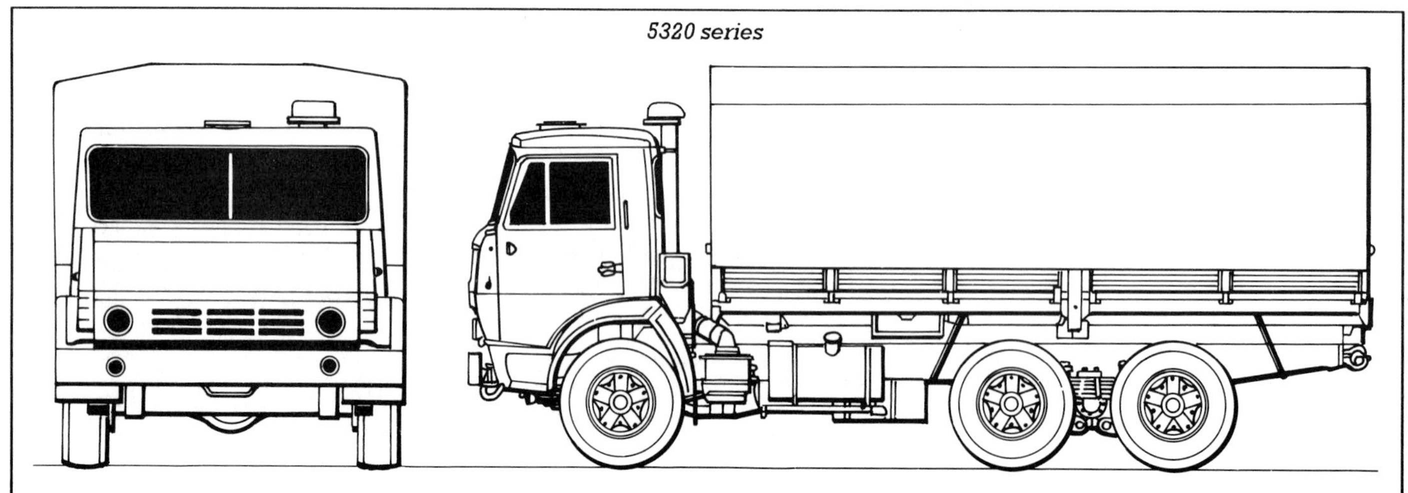
5320 series

Specification

Role: general logistics vehicle
Cab seating: 1 + 2
Configuration: 6 x 4
Weight: (empty) 7080 kg
Max load: 8000 kg
Length: 7.435 m
Width: 2.506 m
Height: 2.83 m
Ground clearance: 0.28 m
Track: 2.026 m/1.856 m
Wheelbase: 3.19 m + 1.32 m
Max speed: (road) 85 km/h
Fuel capacity: approx 400 litres
Fording: 0.5 m
Engine: YaMZ-740 10.85 litre V8 diesel
Power output: 210 hp
Gearbox: manual, 5f, 1r with splitter
Clutch: twin dry plate
Transfer box: none
Steering: mechanical
Turning circle: n/av
Suspension: leaf springs and shock absorbers
Tyres: 12.20 x 400-533
Electrical system: 12 or 24 V

Variants: KamAZ-5320, KamAZ-4310, KamAZ-5410, KamAZ-55102, YaMZ-740, YaMZ-7401

KamAZ-5410 6 x 4 tractor truck

KrAZ - 260 | Former Soviet Union

Production of the **KrAZ-260** began some time during the early 1980s when it replaced the earlier **KrAZ-255B** (qv) on the production lines at the Kremenchug Motor Vehicle Plant. However, the vehicle was not disclosed to the general public until 1985 when examples were displayed towing 152 mm 2A36 nuclear-capable field guns during a Red Square parade - the **KrAZ- 260** can tow loads of up to 10,000 kg when fully loaded (30,000 kg when empty). The Red Square example had an open body equipped with forward-facing bench seats although this may have been a 'parade' configuration. The normal body uses a conventional cargo body with tailgate all covered by the usual tilt over bows. A winch is a standard fitting under the cargo body and can be employed for either forward or rearwards recovery, including self-recovery.

The overall appearance of the **KrAZ-260** is similar to that of the earlier **KrAZ-255B** but the bonnet is more angular to accommodate the turbocharged diesel engine, and the overall dimensions are slightly larger. As far as can be determined the **KrAZ-260** is produced for military service only and as apparently not yet been delivered to armed forces outside the Soviet Union.

Variants known to exist include the **KrAZ-260V** tractor truck, used to tow a variety of semi-trailers, and the **KrAZ- 240**. The latter has a 6 x 4 drive configuration, a slightly longer wheelbase (4.88 m + 1.4 m) and an on-road load capacity of 16,800 kg; it is used for long range logistic support duties, leaving the **KrAZ-260** for forward area load carrying.

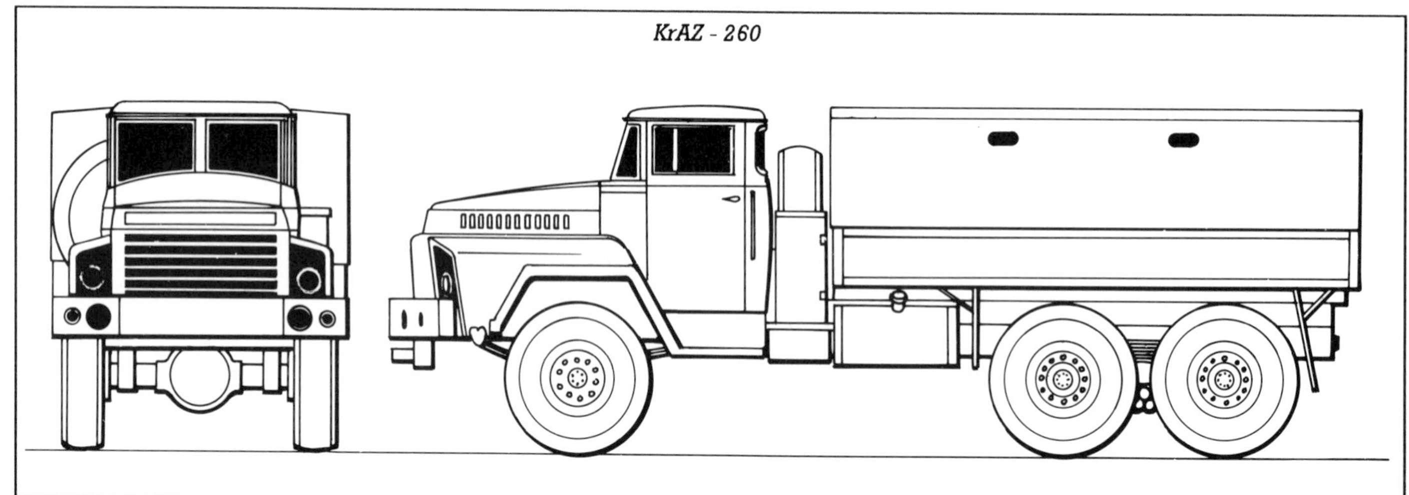
KrAZ - 260

Specification

Role: heavy utility truck
Cab seating: 1 + 2
Configuration: 6 x 6
Weight: (empty) 12,775 kg
Max load: 9000 kg
Length: 10.13 m
Width: 2.722 m
Height: 2.985 m
Ground clearance: 0.37 m
Track: 2.16 m
Wheelbase: 4.6 m + 1.4 m
Max speed: (road) approx 80 km/h
Fuel capacity: 330 litres
Fording: 1.2 m
Engine: YaMZ-238L 14.86 litre V8 turbocharged diesel
Power output: 288 hp/2100 rpm
Gearbox: manual, 8f, 1r
Clutch: single dry plate
Transfer box: 2-speed
Steering: mechanical
Turning circle: 27 m
Suspension: leaf springs and shock absorbers
Tyres: 13.00 x 530-533
Electrical system: 24 V

Variants: KrAZ-260, KrAZ-260V, KrAZ-240

KrAZ-260V tractor truck towing workshop body

ZIL - 135 Series

The first of the **ZIL-135** was produced during the 1960s as a 10 tonne cargo truck for commercial construction use in remote areas such as Siberia. The design was formulated at the Likhachev Motor Vehicle Plant near Moscow so the design has a ZIL prefix but production was carried out at the Bryansk Motor Vehicle Plant. Thus the truck version is known both as the **ZIL-135L4** and the **BAZ-135L4**.

The overall design of the ZIL-135 series is unusual in that it has a forward control cab with two V8 diesel engines in a compartment behind the cab - each engine drives the four wheels on one side via a hydro-mechanical transmission.

Steering is carried out on the 1st and 4th axles, both of which have torsion bar suspension, while the two centre axles are fixed to the chassis. The open cargo area at the rear can be configured to carry pipelines or similar loads for civil construction use but in military service the ZIL-135 series is often used as a missile carrier and re-supply vehicle (carrying extra missiles) for systems such as the FROG long range artillery rocket series and the Sepal cruise missile.

The vehicle is also used as the carrier and re-supply vehicle for the BM-22 220 mm multiple rocket launcher while an Egyptian conversion is used for the SAKR-80 artillery rocket system. Armed versions carrying twin 23 mm cannon were used as makeshift convoy escort vehicles by the Soviet Army in Afghanistan. A **ZIL-135** chassis was used as the basis for the experimental amphibious bridge system known in the West as the ABS(W). The **ZIL-E-135** was an experimental 5- tonne variant intended for use in desert areas or over snow.

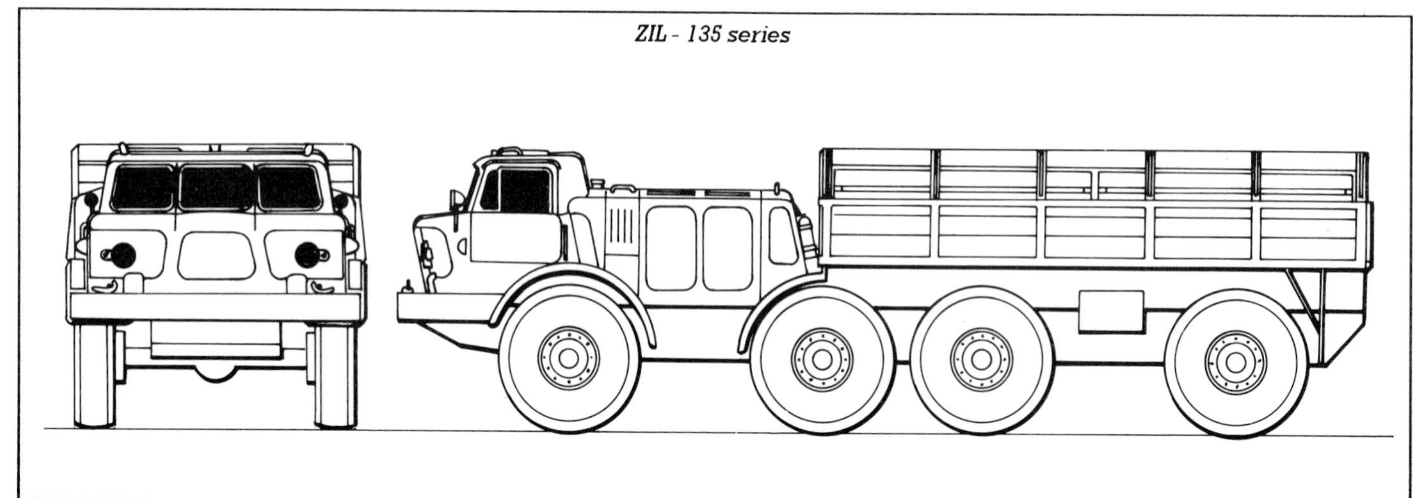

ZIL - 135 series

Specification

Role: heavy high mobility utility truck
Cab seating: 1 + 2
Configuration: 8 x 8
Weight: (empty) 9000 kg
Max load: 10,000 kg
Length: 9.275 m
Width: 2.8 m
Height: 2.53 m
Ground clearance: 0.58 m
Track: 2.3 m
Wheelbase: 2.415 m + 1.5 m + 2.415 m
Max speed: (road) 70 km/h
Fuel capacity: 768 litres
Fording: 0.58 m
Engine: 2 x ZIL-375 7 litre V8 petrol
Power output: each, 180 hp/3200 rpm
Gearbox: hydromechanical transmission, each engine driving four wheels each side
Clutch: none
Transfer box: none
Steering: power assisted on 1st and 4th axles
Turning circle: 25 m
Suspension: 1st and 4th axles torsion bars; 2nd and 3rd axles fixed
Tyres: 16.00 x 20
Electrical system: 24 V

Variants: see text

ZIL-135 8 x 8 truck chassis carrying FROG artillery missiles

MAZ - 537/543 Series Former Soviet Union

The design of the **MAZ-537/543** series began during the early 1960s to produce a heavy load carrier and construction vehicle for use in remote areas. Production of all variants was carried out at the Minsk Motor Vehicle Plant. The **MAZ-537A** emerged as a 15-tonne truck with a central tyre pressure regulation system and powered by a standard tank engine

The 6 tonne **MAZ-535** uses an engine de-rated to 375 hp. The **MAZ-537K**was fitted with a load-handling crane and a version carrying a turntable crane has been reported. Other vehicles in the **MAZ-537** series are in use as tank transporters (qv) and the trucks may be used as heavy artillery tractors. From the **MAZ- 535/537** series the **MAZ-543** evolved as a specialist carrier vehicle which is now used to carry numerous missile and rocket systems such as the SS-1 Scud series, the SS-12 Scaleboard and the SSC-3 coastal defence missile.

Other vehicles are used as command and erector vehicles for the SA-10 Grumble missile system. Other variants of the basic series which appeared during the mid-1970s include the later MAZ-7310 cargo truck, the MAZ- 7510 dump truck, and the MAZ-7910 pipeline carrier.

An aircraft crash tender, the **AA-60 (7310)-160.1**, has also been produced. All these vehicles have forward control cabs, some versions using separate compartments on each side of the engine, each with tandem seating for two. Standard equipment includes an engine pre-heater and powerful cab heaters. At least one experimental variant powered by a 1100 hp gas turbine has been developed for trials.

MAZ - 537/543 series

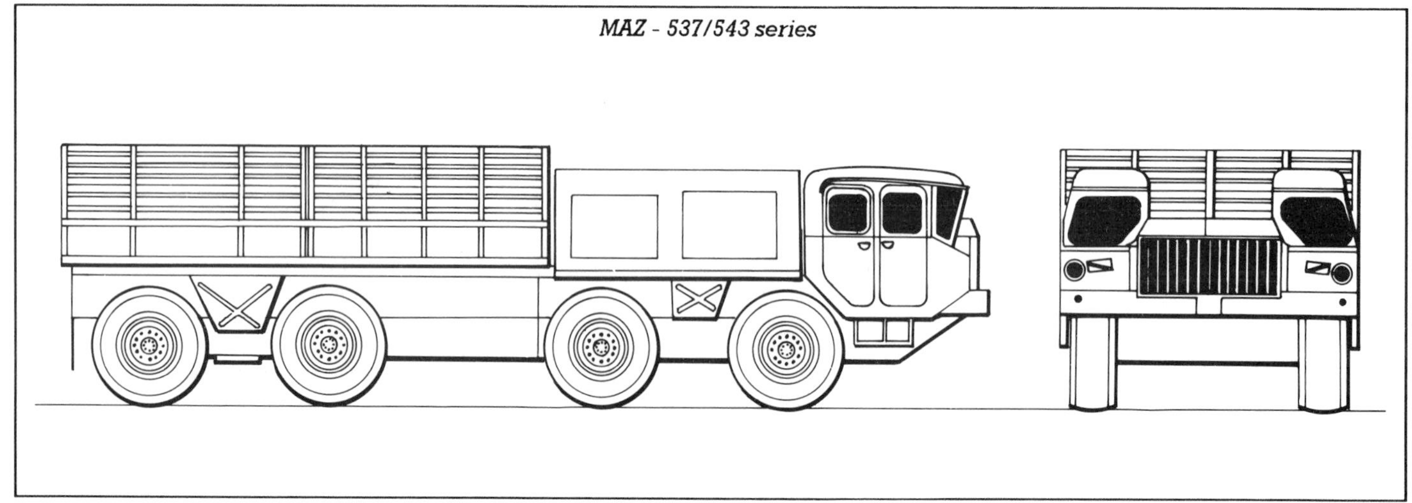

Specification

MAZ-543

Role: heavy high mobility utility trucks
Cab seating: 1 + 3
Configuration: 8 x 8
Weight: (empty) 17,300 kg
Max load: 15,000 kg
Length: 11.7 m
Width: 2.98 m
Height: 2.925 m
Ground clearance: 0.45 m
Track: 2.375 m
Wheelbase: 2.2 m + 3.3 m + 2.2 m
Max speed: (road) approx 60 km/h
Fuel capacity: n/av
Fording: 1 m
Engine: D12A-525 38.9 litre V12 diesel
Power output: 525 hp/2100 rpm
Gearbox: hydro-mechanical transmission
Clutch: none
Transfer box: none
Steering: power assisted on front four wheels
Turning circle: n/av
Suspension: torsion bar
Tyres: 15.00 x 23.5
Electrical system: 24 V

Variants: MAZ-535, MAZ-537A, MAZ-537K, MAZ-543, MAZ-7310, MAZ- 7510, MAZ-7910, also see text

MAZ-543 8 x 8 truck chassis being used for BM-22 220 mm multiple rocket system

URO 115 PM

Spain

The firm of URO Vehiculos Especiales SA was formed in 1981 to produce a new series of commercial trucks which were manufactured in four versions. One of them, the **U-12.13** was selected to enter a competition to determine a new light utility vehicle for the Spanish armed forces. The trials were completed in 1983 and the URO entry, the **URO 115 PM** was selected and ordered during late 1984. The type is now in production at Santiago de Compostella, making use of many URO-designed and manufactured components such as the axles and transfer box.

In design terms the **URO 115 PM** is entirely conventional with the engine mounted over the front axle. It uses a forward-tilting and forward control cab with provision for roof hatches; glass reinforced plastic panels are mounted on a steel tube frame. The cargo area may be covered by tilt over bows but is more often left open. Removing the drop sides and tailgate allows ISO shelters and containers to be carried. Two wheelbase lengths are produced, 2.8 m and 3.2 m, both with the same payload capacity.

Numerous special bodies can be fitted including the usual fuel and water tankers, mobile workshops, fire and crash tenders, and a four-stretcher ambulance.

Proposed versions include a 16-seater minibus, a light recovery vehicle and a deep wading variant.

Panel-bodied vans could be used for telecommunications and command posts. Most of the special bodies are used on the long wheelbase model.

A winch may be fitted to the front of any variant.

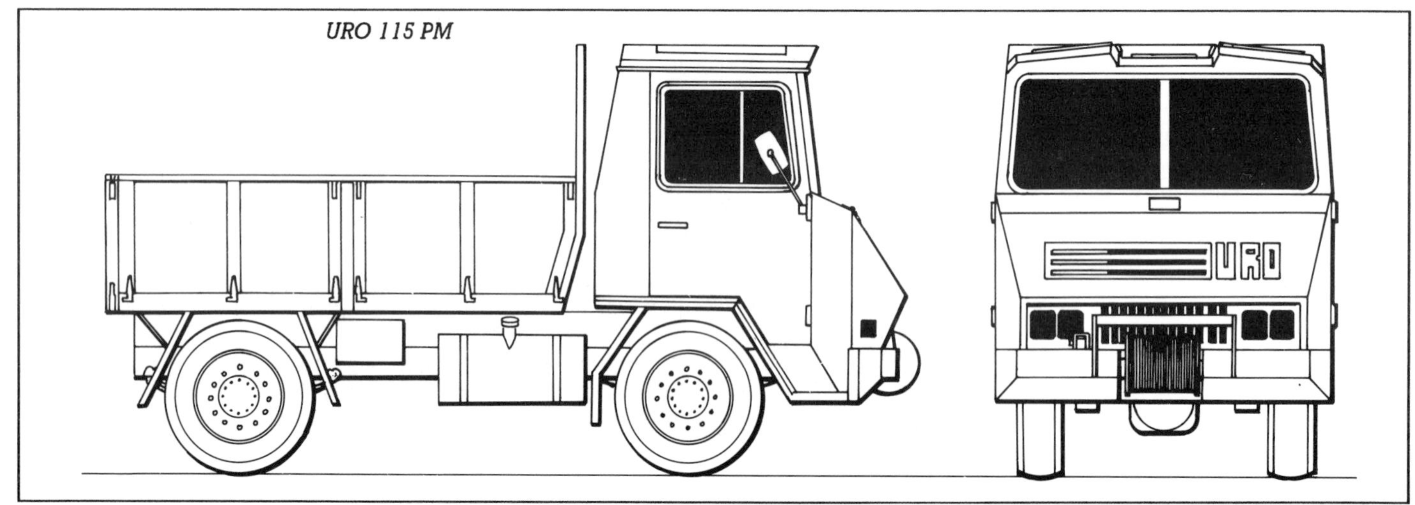

URO 115 PM

Specification

Role: light utility truck
Cab seating: 1 + 1
Configuration: 4 x 4
Weight: (empty) 9900 kg
Max load: 2000 kg
Length: 4.915 m or 5.315 m
Width: 1.985 m
Height: 2.55 m
Ground clearance: 0.38 m
Track: 1.555 m
Wheelbase: 2.8 m or 3.2 m
Max speed: (road) 96 km/h
Fuel capacity: 180 litres
Fording: 0.8 m
Engine: Perkins Iberica 6.354.3 5.8 litre 6 cylinder diesel
Power output: 118 hp
Gearbox: manual, 5f, 1r
Clutch: single dry plate
Transfer box: URO URT-1 2-speed
Steering: hydraulic power assisted
Turning circle: 14.3 m or 16 m
Suspension: leaf springs with shock absorbers
Tyres: 13.80 x 20
Electrical system: 24 V

Variants: see text

URO 115 PM 4 x 4 2-tonne truck

Pegaso 3055 Spain

The **Pegaso 3055** is a 6 x 6 development of the **Pegaso 3046** (qv) and has a nominal on-road payload of 10 tonnes. It shares many components with the **Pegaso 3046** series, including the cab.

The **Pegaso 3055** was produced primarily for the Spanish armed forces with whom it is the standard vehicle in its class. Apart from the basic cargo version, which can carry up to 30 troops in the cargo area, the **Pegaso 3055** is used as the carrier vehicle for the Teruel multiple launcher artillery rocket system, and as a tractor truck for towing tank-carrying semi-trailers.

Other variants include a heavy recovery vehicle with a swivelling crane, refrigerated cold storage vehicles, fuel and water tankers, and van-bodied variants for use as command vehicles and mobile offices. The basic chassis is also used to carry heavy combat engineering equipment such as bridging sections. Some vehicles carry a winch.

In 1987 the **Pegaso 3055** was replaced in production by the **Pegaso 7323** which is similar to the earlier model other than the installation of a naturally aspirated 10.52 litre diesel developing 225 hp, a longer wheelbase (3.7 m + 1.484 m), and a revised drive train employing ZF components.

The Pegaso 7323 has been adopted by the Spanish armed forces and over 1,000 were sold to Morocco. It involves the same variants as the **Pegaso 3055** but new versions include an artillery tractor for 155 mm howitzers, a front-line ambulance, a tipper truck and a fire tender.

Optional equipment for the 3046 and 7323 includes a deep wading kit (up to 1.9 m), a hard-top cab a power take-off on the transfer case, increased capacity or extra fuel tanks, and other sizes of tyres including run-flats.

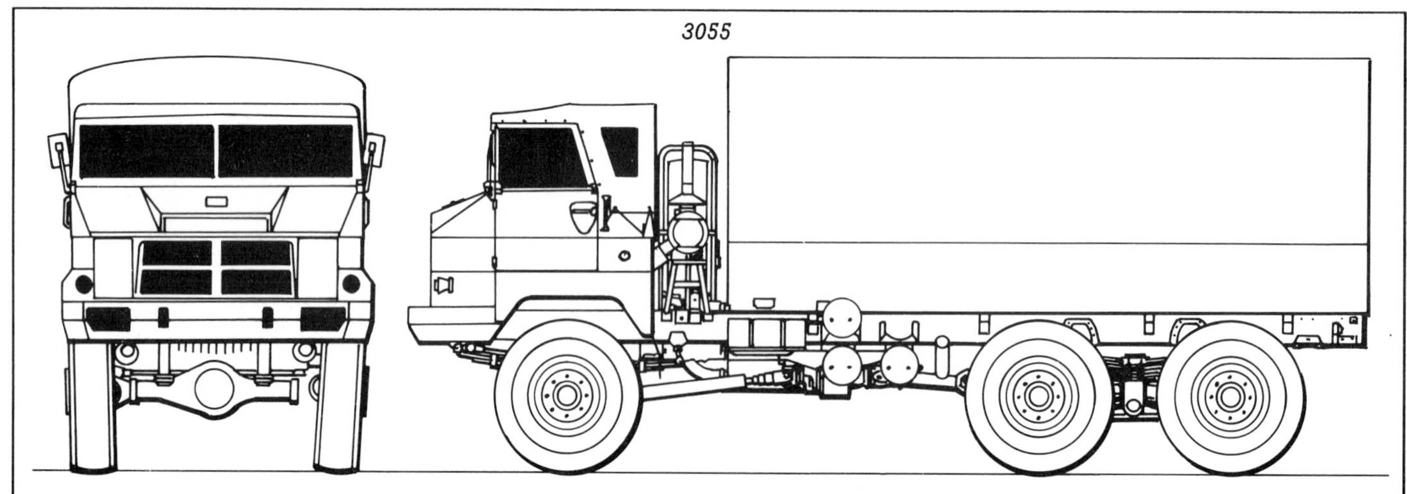

Specification

Role: heavy utility truck
Cab seating: 1 + 1
Configuration: 6 x 6
Weight: (empty) 9000 kg
Max load: 6000 kg
Length: 6.956 m
Width: 2.4 m
Height: 2.71 m
Ground clearance: 0.34 m
Track: 1.96 m
Wheelbase: 3.245 m + 1.484 m
Max speed: (road) 80 km/h
Fuel capacity: 360 litres
Fording: 1.1 m
Engine: Pegaso 10.52 litre 6 cylinder turbocharged diesel
Power output: 220 hp/2000 rpm
Gearbox: Pegaso manual, 6f, 1r
Clutch: Pegaso single dry plate
Transfer box: Pegaso 2-speed
Steering: recirculating ball, power assisted
Turning circle: 22.2 m
Suspension: Leaf springs and shock absorbers
Tyres: 13.00 x 20 or 14.00 x 20
Electrical system: 24 V

Variants: 3046, 3055, 7323

Pegaso 3055 6 x 6 6-tonne truck

Volvo 4140 Sweden

Development of the Volvo 4140 series began in 1966 when Volvo were awarded a contract to develop a new high mobility family of tactical vehicles with both 4 x 4 and 6 x 6 drive configurations. The 4 x 4 became the **Volvo 4141** (or **C303**) and the 6 x 6 the **Volvo 4143** (or **C306**); the 4 x 4 **Volvo C304** has a slightly longer wheelbase (2.53 m). Also developed at the same time was a 6 x 6 amphibious variant and an 8 x 8 model; neither of which got past the prototype stage.

The 4 x 4 version emerged as a 1.2 tonne nominal payload vehicle and the 6 x 6 as a 2.4 tonne. While both are still used as light utility cargo vehicles they are more often used as fully-enclosed personnel or equipment carriers.

Both vehicles use identical front ends as they share the same engine, gearbox, transfer box and cab.

The cargo area may be protected by a canvas tilt but due to the harsh Swedish climate many vehicles use hard-topped bodies equipped with powerful heaters.

The 4 x 4 models can seat up to six troops, the 8 x 8 up to ten. Both configurations are used as radio link, ambulance, command, radio and multi-purpose vehicles. These vehicles are mainly used by the Swedish armed forces but some were supplied to Malaysia. Some were sold commercially.

The Volvo 4140 series is now out of production.

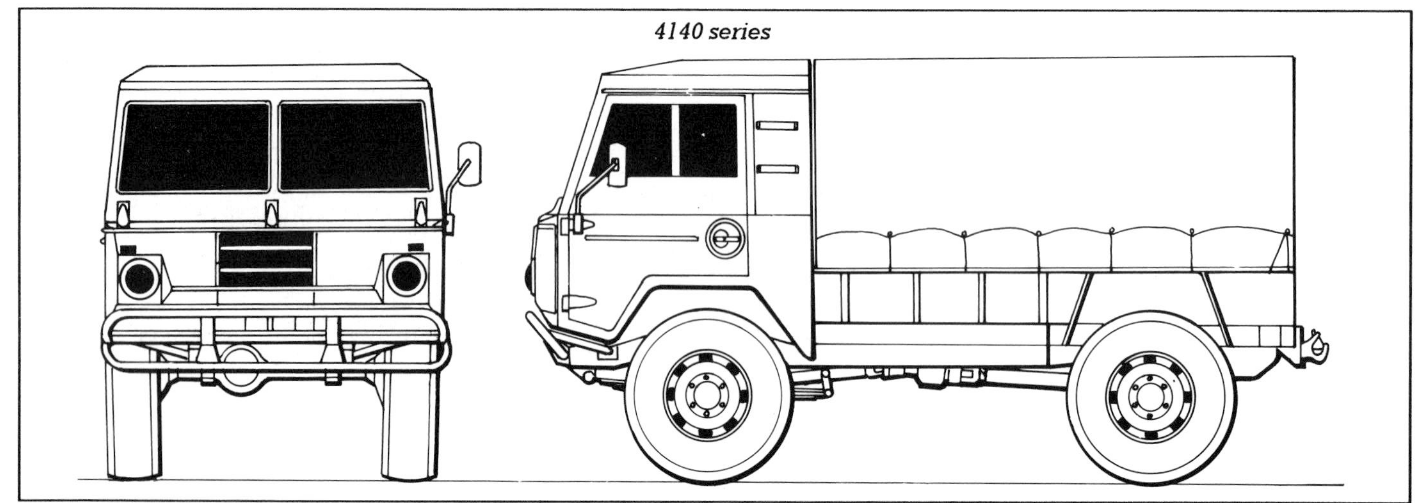

4140 series

Specification

Data for C306 6 x 6

Role: light utility vehicle
Cab seating: 1 + 1
Configuration: 6 x 6
Weight: (empty) 2400 kg
Max load: 3100 kg
Length: 5.735 m
Width: 1.88 m
Height: 2.13 m
Ground clearance: 0.386 m
Track: 1.54 m
Wheelbase: 2.72 m + 1.05 m
Max speed: (road) 90 km/h
Fuel capacity: 150 litres
Fording: 0.7 m
Engine: Volvo B-30 2.98 litre 6 cylinder petrol
Power output: 125 hp/4250 rpm
Gearbox: Volvo M 400 manual, 4f, 1r
Clutch: single dry plate
Transfer box: Volvo G5 2-speed
Steering: ZF cam and roller
Turning circle: 16.5 m
Suspension: leaf springs and shock absorbers
Tyres: 8.90 x 16
Electrical system: 12 V

Variants: C303, C304, C306, 4141, 4143

Volvo 4143, the 6 x 6 version of the Volvo 4140 series

Saab-Scania SBA 111 and SBAT 111S Sweden

Design work on the **Saab-Scania SBA 111** 4 x 4 and **SBAT 111S** 6 x 6 trucks began during the late 1960s and the first prototypes appeared during 1971; production commenced in 1976.

The two vehicles were designed to be the main tactical trucks of the Swedish armed forces and over 2500 were delivered to the Swedish Army alone, more went to the Swedish air force and navy. The two vehicles share many components (there is 90% parts commonality), such as the forward control cab, with the main difference, apart from the extra axle and enlarged cargo area, being that the 6 x 6 uses a turbocharged engine.

In both 4 x 4 and 6 x 6 versions, the cargo carrier is the main version, the 4 x 4 being able to carry 4500 kg across country and the 6 x 6 6000 kg; road payloads are 6000 kg and 9000 kg respectively. Hydraulic materials handling cranes are fitted to some vehicles. Numbers of **SBAT 111S** trucks are used to tow 155 mm FH-77A field howitzers and 120 mm KARIN coast defence guns; at least 600 slightly modified **SBAT 111S** trucks have been exported to India to tow and support 155 mm FH-77B field howitzers. The artillery tractors have a crew shelter on the cargo area.

Other variants include **SBAT 111S** chassis modified to carry shelters for the Giraffe radar system; these vehicles have four stabiliser jacks which are lowered when the radar arm is elevated. Crash rescue variants are used by the Royal Swedish Air Force and **SBA 111**s are used by the same service for snow clearing. Finland also uses a small number of 4 x 4 **SBA 111**s.

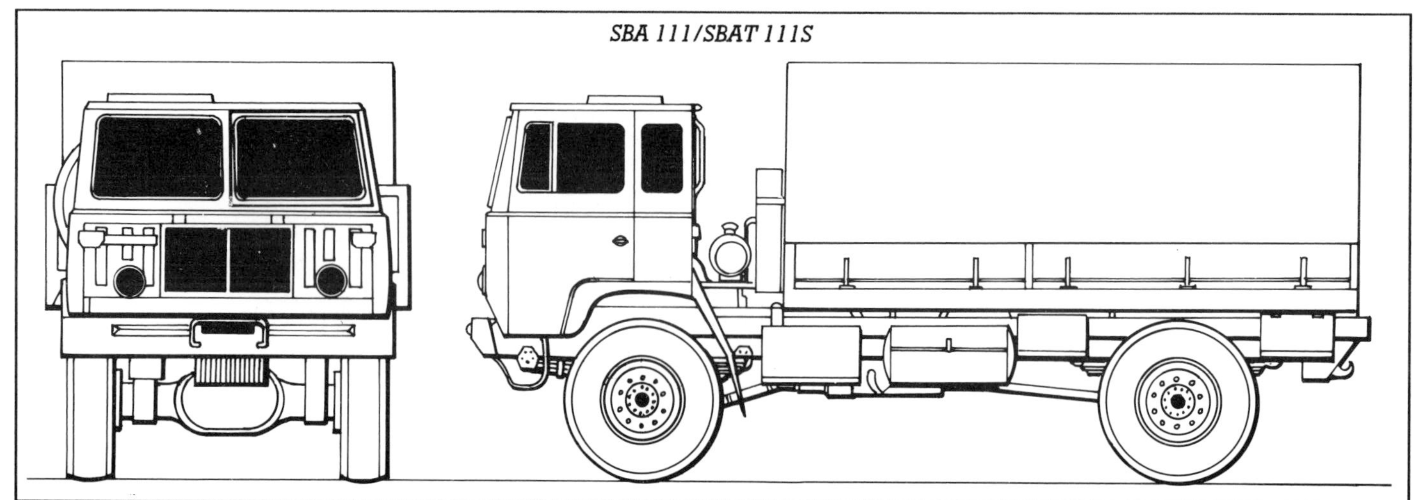

SBA 111/SBAT 111S

Specification

Specification of SBAT 111S

Role: general utility truck and artillery tractor
Cab seating: 1 + 2
Configuration: 6 x 6
Weight: (empty) 11650 kg
Max load: 6000 kg
Length: 7.78 m
Width: 2.48 m
Height: 2.9 m
Ground clearance: 0.42 m
Track: 2.02 m
Wheelbase: 3.55 m + 1.48 m
Max speed: (road) 85 km/h
Fuel capacity: 167 litres
Fording: 0.8 m
Engine: Scania DS11LB27 11 litre 6 cylinder supercharged diesel
Power output: 296 hp/2200 rpm
Gearbox: automatic, 6f, 1r
Clutch: none - torque converter
Transfer box: 2-speed
Steering: hydraulic
Turning circle: 20.6 m
Suspension: leaf springs with shock absorbers
Tyres: 14.00 x 20
Electrical system: 24 V

Variants: see text

Scania SBA 111S 6 x 6 truck towing dummy gun during trials

Bedford M Series **UK**

The **Bedford M series** was a logical development of the earlier **Bedford RL** series carried out during the early 1960s and intended to replace the RL, the design of which dated back to the early 1950s.

The largest customer by far for the M series was the British Army for whom the vehicle is known simply as the 4-tonner, even though the maximum load possible is over 6 tonnes. The initial models were known as the **MK**, powered by a multi-fuel engine, but the introduction of a more powerful diesel engine after 1981 resulted in the MJ series. In its basic form the M series truck is a forward control cab design, with or without a winch, and with removable cargo drop sides and a tailgate. Outside Europe the canvas tilt and bows are often removed. The M series are true multi-purpose vehicles being used for all manner of military duties including personnel carriers, artillery tractors, tippers, snow ploughs, reconnaissance drone carriers, fuel pack carriers, signals vehicles, light recovery, artillery control centres, portable roadway carriers and layers, bridging trucks, and so on. The RAF uses them to support Harrier operations and the Royal Navy also operates a sizeable fleet. The Saxon armoured personnel carrier uses many M-series components.

Many M-series trucks have been exported to nations such as Kenya and Bangladesh. The selection of a Leyland Trucks design as the M-series replacement will not mean that the M series trucks will vanish from British service. That will not take place for many years yet as production continued until the end of 1989. By then the old Bedford concern had become AWD Bedford, later taken over by Marshalls of Cambridge where production to order is now carried out. Late production trucks can be recognised by the platform over the cab roof.

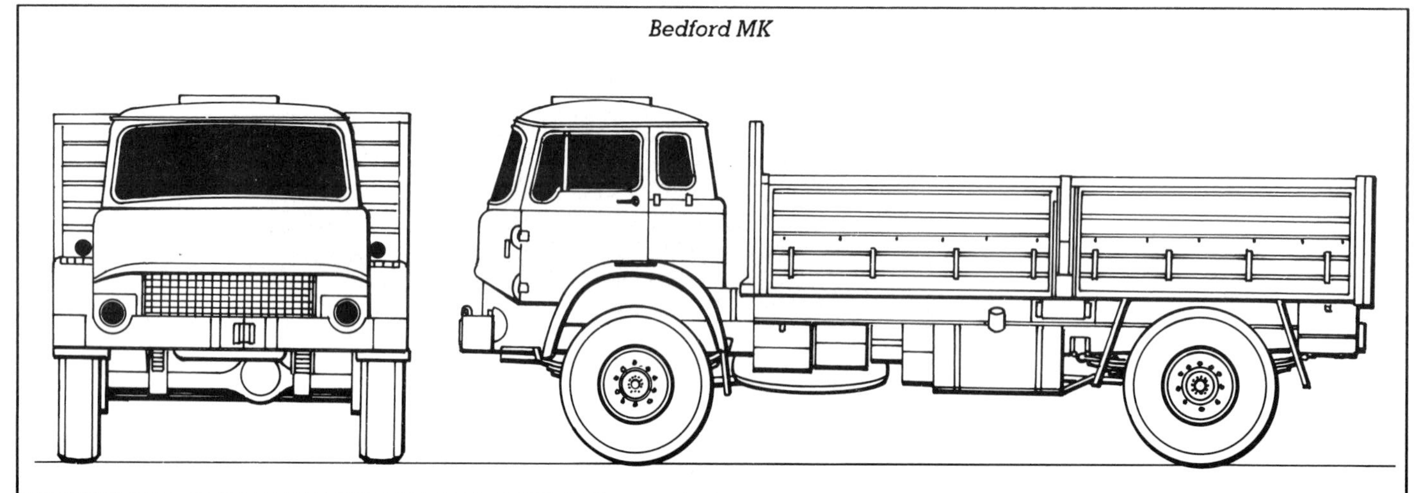
Bedford MK

Specification

Role: General utility truck
Cab seating: 1 + 1
Configuration: 4 x 4
Weight: (empty) 5130 kg
Max load: 4000 kg
Length: 6.58 m
Width: 2.489 m
Height: 2.5 m
Ground clearance: 0.343 m
Track: 2.05 m/2.03 m
Wheelbase: 3.962 m
Max speed: (road) 77 km/h
Fuel capacity: 155 litres
Fording: 0.762 m
Engine: Bedford 5.42 litre 6-cylinder diesel
Power output: 98 hp/2600 rpm
Gearbox: manual, 4f 1r
Clutch: single dry plate
Transfer box: 2-speed
Steering: worm and sector
Turning circle: 18 m
Suspension: semi-elliptic leaf springs and shock absorbers
Tyres: 12.00 x 20 (or others)
Electrical system: 24 V

Variants: See text

Bedford M-series 4 x 4, 4 tonne trucks carrying communication equipment shelters

Bedford TM 4-4 and TM 6-6 UK

The **TM 4-4** and **TM 6-6** trucks are two basically similar trucks, the **TM 4-4** being a 4 x 4, 8 tonne vehicle and the **TM 6-6** being a 6 x 6, 14 tonne design (maximum load 16 tonnes). They share many components in common, such as the utilitarian forward control cab and engine, while many design details, such as the cargo area loading heights, are identical on both vehicles. However the **TM 4-4** uses a Spicer transmission and the **TM 6-6** a ZF S6-80 (and an exhaust brake).

The **TM 4-4** was developed first in answer to a British Army requirement issued during the early 1970s - the first production examples were delivered in 1981. The **TM 6-6** followed with production commencing in 1986.

Production of both models has now ceased with over 2100 **TM 4-4s** and 1045 **TM 6-6s** being built.

Small numbers of both vehicles were exported to the Middle East, the **TM 6-6s** involved being fitted with Cummins engines.

The basic form of both vehicles is a flat bed cargo vehicle capable of carrying standard NATO ammunition or other stores-carrying pallets. For this role both vehicles can be fitted with self-loading hydraulic cranes located behind the cab. Standard shelters or workshop bodies may also be carried. Drop sides and a tailgate can be added to convert the vehicles into general load carriers.

Seating for personnel may also be fitted. Centrally-mounted winches are mounted on some vehicles.

A tipper version of the **TM 4-4** is in service.

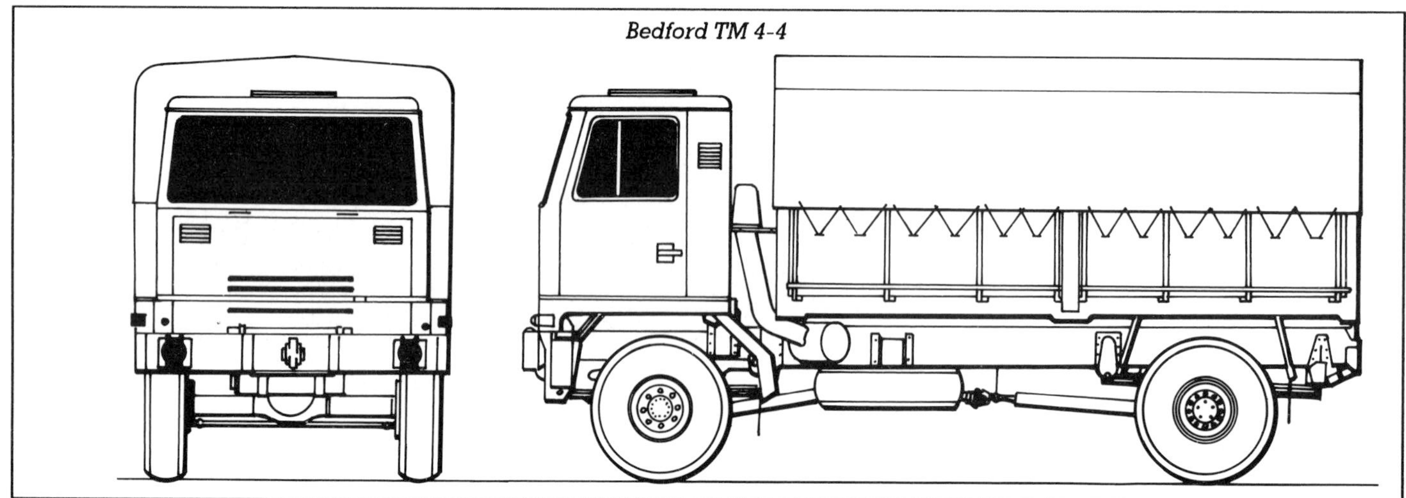

Bedford TM 4-4

Specification

Data for TM 4-4

Role: Heavy utility truck
Cab seating: 1 + 1
Configuration: 4 x 4
Weight: (empty) 8300 kg
Max load: 8000 kg
Length: 6.623 m
Width: 2.476 m
Height: 2.997 m
Ground clearance: 0.352 m
Track: 2.02 m/2.08 m
Wheelbase: 4.325 m
Max speed: (road) 93 km/h
Fuel capacity: 155 litres
Fording: 0.75 m
Engine: Bedford 8.2/205 TD 8.2 litre diesel
Power output: 206 hp/2500 rpm
Gearbox: Spicer T6 manual, 6f, 1r
Clutch: twin dry plate
Transfer box: 2-speed
Steering: recirculating ball, power assisted
Turning circle: 17.5 m
Suspension: taper leaf springs with shock absorbers
Tyres: 15.50/80 x 20
Electrical system: 24 V

Variants: see text

Bedford TM 6-6 flatbed trucks carrying bridging equipment

Leyland 4 tonne Truck — UK

In June 1989 the **Leyland DAF 4-tonne Truck** was selected to be the basis of the next generation of 4-tonne trucks used by the British Army. The selection followed an arduous 'drive off' contest against designs from AWD Bedford and Volvo Trucks (GB) Limited and the initial order was for 5350 units. The Leyland entrant, now produced by Leyland Trucks, was based on a design known initially as the **T.244**, an entirely orthodox design with a forward control all-steel cab and a conventional cargo body with a removable tailgate and dropsides. The forward-tilting cab design was based on the C.44 used on the Leyland Roadrunner commercial light truck and is so arranged to allow the vehicle to be driven directly into a C-130 Hercules transport aircraft. The cab interior has space to allow it to be used for driver training or to allow radios to be installed, in addition to the space provision for the crew's kit. Every component on the vehicle was rigorously tested prior to the selection contest, including the axles which were specially developed at the Leyland Albion plant in Glasgow.

The Leyland truck has assumed many of the tasks undertaken by in-service 4-tonne vehicles. These roles include flat-bed versions used to carry Medium Girder Bridge sections, a field refuelling module, various types of ISO containers for electronics and communication systems, workshops, and acting as a mobile trackway carrier and layer. It is anticipated that a recovery version will be developed. Optional equipment includes a front or rear-operating winch, left or right-hand drive, a tipper body, and a load-handling crane.

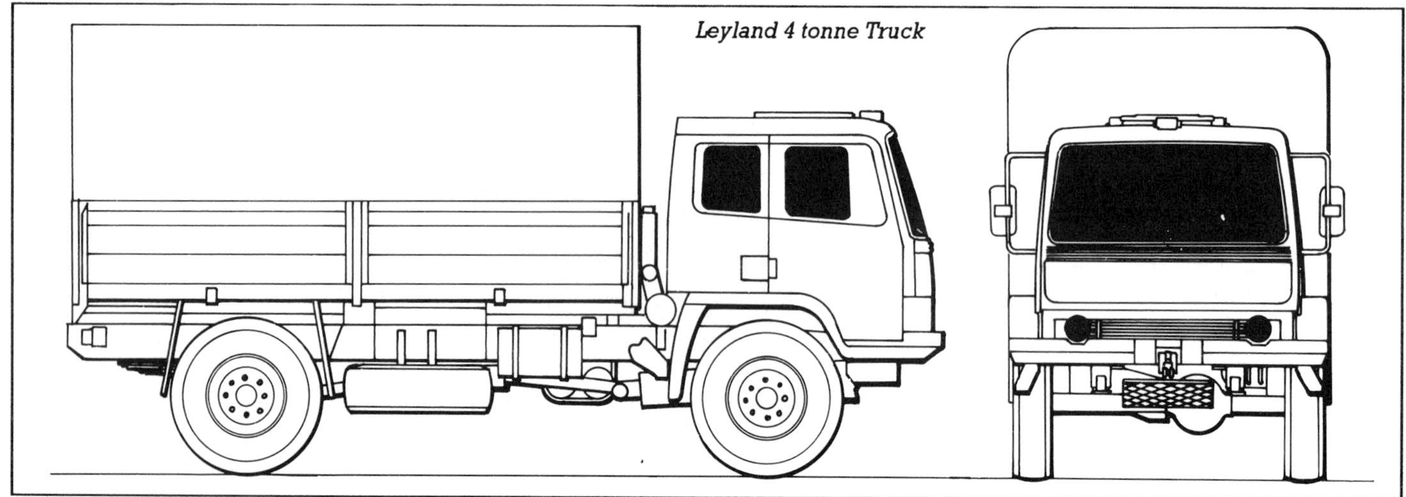

Leyland 4 tonne Truck

Specification

Role: general utility truck
Cab seating: 1 + 2
Configuration: 4 x 4 (permanent)
Weight: (empty) 6010 kg
Max load: 4200 kg
Length: 6.65 m
Width: 2.49 m
Height: 3.34 m
Ground clearance: 0.32 m
Track: 2.1 m
Wheelbase: 3.95 m
Max speed: (road) 89 km/h
Fuel capacity: 135 litres
Fording: 0.75 m
Engine: Leyland 310 5.9 litre 6 cylinder turbocharged diesel
Power output: 145 hp/2600 rpm
Gearbox: Turner T5-350 synchromesh, 5f, 1r
Clutch: single dry plate
Transfer box: Getrag 305 2-speed
Steering: ZF 8045 power assisted
Turning circle: 18 m
Suspension: taper leaf springs with shock absorbers
Tyres: 12.00 R 20
Electrical system: 24 V

Variants: see text

Leyland Truck 4-tonne truck prototype undergoing durability trials

CUCV

USA

By 1980 the US Armed Forces found themselves using a wide variety of light vehicles for numerous tactical and other applications that often overlapped, and many of which were too expensive to run and maintain. A study was instituted to cut down the number of vehicle types in service and replace them with relatively low-cost militarised commercial types. The result was the Commercial Utility Cargo Vehicle (CUCV) programme. Following a series of trials, General Motors were awarded a massive contract in 1982 for no less than 53,000 plus Model K pick-up trucks to be produced in five basic forms.

The basic Model K was provided with only the minimum of alterations to make it suitable for military use. The basic CUCV is the **M1009**, a utility personnel run-about with a 2.705 metre wheelbase; all the other versions have a 3.34 metre wheelbase. The **M1008** is a general cargo pick-up truck with an open cargo area, while the **M1010** is a four-stretcher ambulance with a box body. The **M1028** is equipped to carry light tactical shelters for communications or other equipment and the **M1031** is a 1.25 ton light truck.

All these vehicles use the same components such as the basic chassis, engine, transmission, axles and electrical system (the ambulance version has a revised electrical system).

The CUCV series has been widely issued throughout the American armed forces, where it has replaced many old Jeeps and other vehicle models, and has been exported to nations such as Jamaica and Liberia. Well over 70,000 had been manufactured when production ceased.

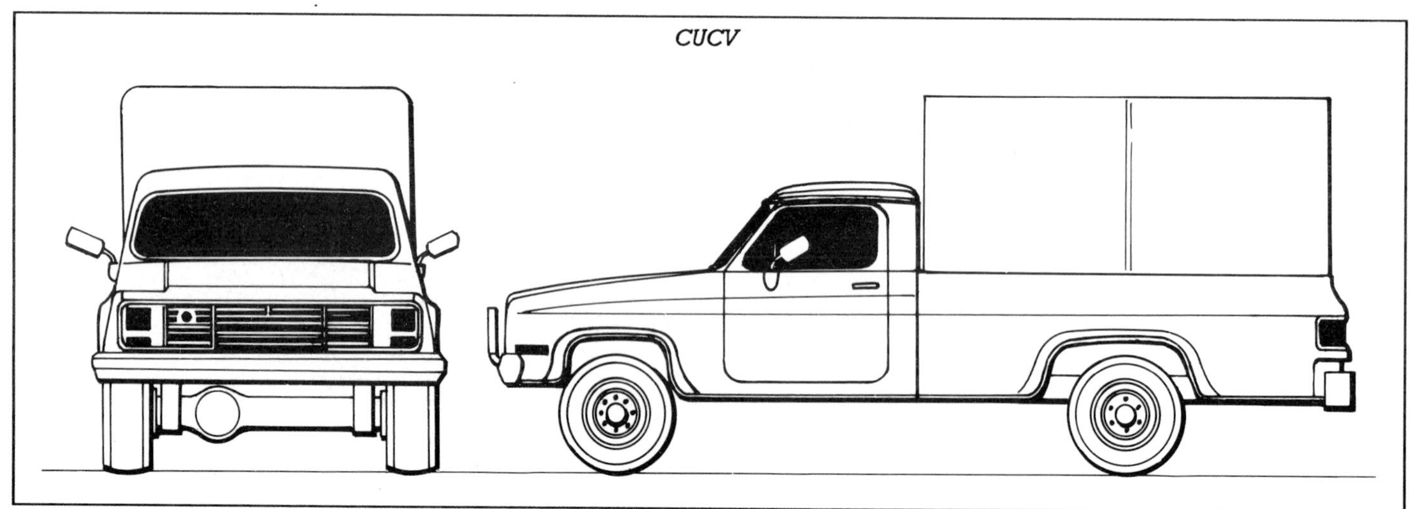
CUCV

Specification
Data for M1009

Role: utility vehicles
Cab seating: 1 + 1 or 2
Configuration: 4 x 4
Weight: (empty) 2360 kg
Max load: 544 kg
Length: 4.873 m
Width: 2.022 m
Height: 1.905 m
Ground clearance: 0.21 m
Track: 1.485 m/1.38 m
Wheelbase: 2.705 m
Max speed: (road) 80 km/h
Fuel capacity: 90 litres
Fording: 0.5 m
Engine: GM 6.2 litre V8 diesel
Power output: 135 hp/3600 rpm
Gearbox: GM automatic, 3f, 1r
Clutch: single dry plate
Transfer box: 2-speed
Steering: recirculating ball
Turning circle: 14.6 m
Suspension: leaf springs and shock absorbers
Tyres: 10.00 x 15
Electrical system: 24 V

Variants: M1008, M1009, M1010, M1028, M1030

M1008 CUCV in general cargo form

HMMWV

USA

The High Mobility Multi-purpose Wheeled Vehicle (**HMMWV**) had its origins in a US Army requirement drafted during the late 1970s. Following exhaustive testing of models from three manufacturers, the AM General submission was selected for production with an initial five-year contract for no less than 54,973 units - a later follow-on contract involved a further 33,000 by 1993. The **HMMWV** is exactly what its name implies, an extremely high mobility vehicle that can traverse almost any type of terrain due to its independent arm suspension on each wheel station and the power of its Detroit Diesel engine.

The base model for what is now a very long list of variants (with more to come) can be taken as the **M998**, a cargo/troops carrier with four occupants seated two each side of the engine housing in the centre. There is space at the rear for cargo. From that base come many variants, including weapon carriers (TOW, machine guns, grenade launchers, surface-to-air missiles, etc), tractors for light artillery, ambulances, resupply vehicles, command and communication shelter carriers, light pick-up trucks, and so on.

To confuse matters further a series of conversion kits can readily transform one variant into another. The **HMMWV**, sometimes known as the **'Hummer'**, has evolved into a well-liked and reliable vehicle. Export sales have been made to Thailand, Taiwan, Luxembourg, Abu Dhabi, the Philippines and Djibuti, among others.

Production is set to continue at the AM General facility at Mishawaka, Indiana, for years to come.

Many old Jeeps and other vehicles have already been replaced by the versatile **HMMWV** and those remaining are scheduled to go sometime soon.

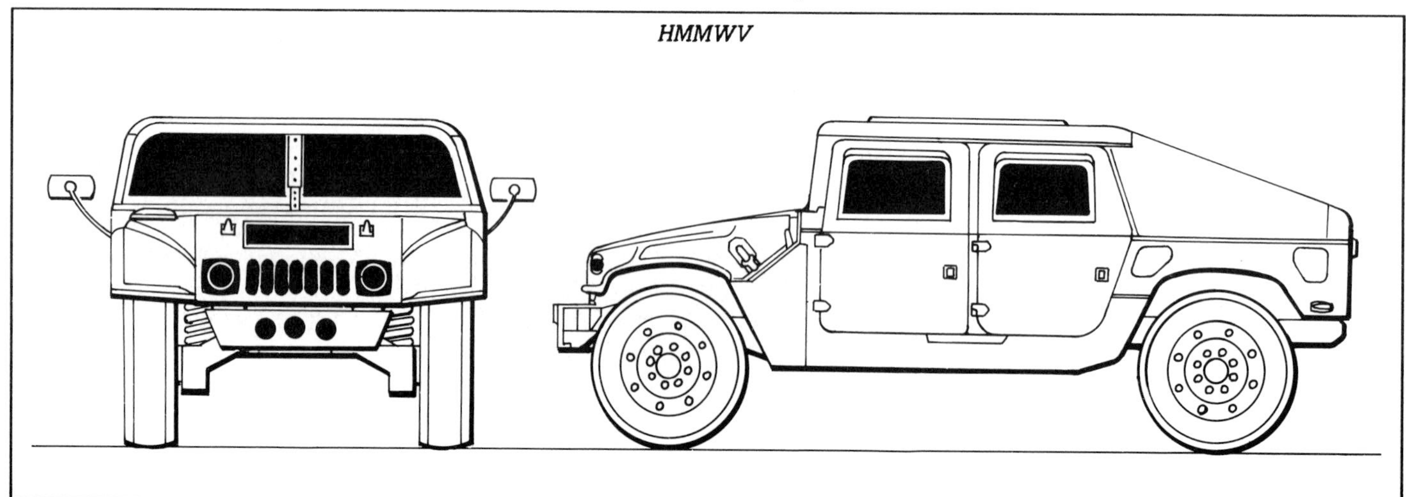

HMMWV

Specification

Role: general purpose high mobility vehicle
Cab seating: 1 + 3
Configuration: 4 x 4
Weight: (empty) 2295 kg
Max load: 1135 kg
Length: 4.57 m
Width: 2.15 m
Height: 1.75 m
Ground clearance: 0.406 m
Track: 1.81 m
Wheelbase: 3.3 m
Max speed: (road) 105 km/h
Fuel capacity: 94 litres
Fording: 0.76 m
Engine: Detroit Diesel 6.2 litre V8 diesel
Power output: 130 hp/3600 rpm
Gearbox: automatic, 3f, 1r
Clutch: single dry plate
Transfer box: 2-speed
Steering: power assisted
Turning circle: 14.63 m
Suspension: independent A-arms and coil springs
Tyres: 36 x 12.5-16.5
Electrical system: 24 V

Variants: many, see text

M998 HMMWV armed with 30 mm cannon

M35 Truck Series

The **AM General M35 series**, sometimes referred to as the M44 series from another model in the same range, dates back to truck designs produced in the late 1940s and based on WW2 experience.

The series evolved from a number of designs from several concerns rather than a single source, for AM General took over many companies such as Reo and Kaiser Jeep who produced similar vehicles. Originally petrol engines were used but this was switched to diesel from 1973 onwards.

The number of variants in the series, all based on a number of 2.5 ton cargo trucks, has risen to an alarming number and new variants continue to appear, even though production of the series had ceased by 1989.

A listing of variants is too long to reproduce in these pages for each variant was seemingly produced in several versions and in some cases chassis intended for one variant was used by another. Included in the **M35** series are basic 2.5 ton cargo trucks, some with single rear wheels some with double, some with winches, some without, and so on. Then there are fuel and water tankers, tippers, van-bodied trucks, recovery vehicles, tractor trucks with fifth wheels, workshop and maintenance trucks, medical vans, engineer vehicles, and so on.

To add to the list are numerous kits for deep wading, arctic use, personnel seating, and many others.

Under it all the **M35** series still retains the 'classic' American service truck appearance and layout with a fuel-hungry engine, a soft-topped cab (often replaced by a hard top) and a seemingly small load for the size of chassis. At one time in the early 1980s the US Army alone had well over 63,000 **M35** series trucks. They are due to be replaced by the 4 x 4 component of the projected Family of Medium Tactical Vehicles (FMTV).

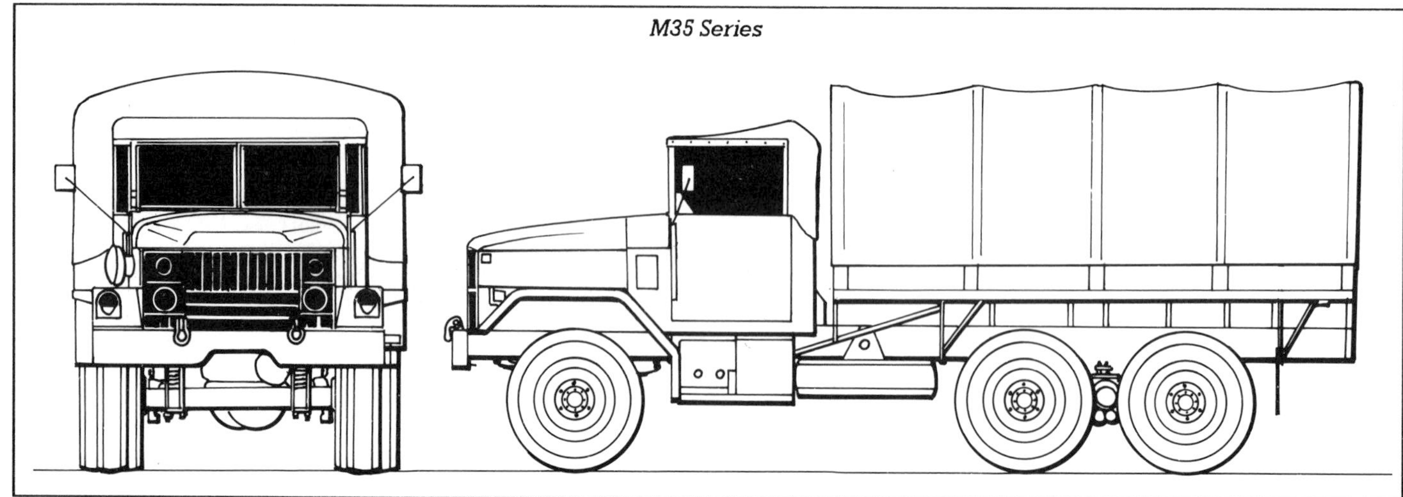

M35 Series

Specification

Role: general utility truck
Cab seating: 1 + 1 or 2
Configuration: 6 x 6
Weight: (empty) 5900 kg
Max load: 2268 kg
Length: 6.7 m
Width: 2.4 m
Height: 2.9 m
Ground clearance: 0.28 m
Track: 1.72 m/1.778 m
Wheelbase: 3.912 m
Max speed: (road) 90 km/h
Fuel capacity: 189 litres
Fording: 0.76 m
Engine: LDT-465-1C 7.8 litre 6-cylinder multi-fuel diesel
Power output: 140 hp/2600 rpm
Gearbox: manual, 5f, 1r
Clutch: single dry plate
Transfer box: 2-speed
Steering: cam and twin lever
Turning circle: 22 m
Suspension: leaf springs, inverted at rear
Tyres: 9.00 x 20
Electrical system: 24 V

Variants: many, see text

M49 fuel tanker, one of many M35 6 x 6 truck variants

M809 Series

The **M809** series of 5 ton trucks was based on a design that entered production in 1950 and remained in production for over 30 years.

The original M54 series of the 1950s used petrol engines but by 1970 the switch to diesel was made and the **M809** series began. The M809 referred to the chassis type (there were also M810, M811 and M812 chassis) and the series included the **M813** cargo truck (the **M813A1** had drop sides), the long wheelbase **M814** cargo truck, the **M815** bolster truck, the **M817** tipper, the **M818** tractor truck, the **M820** van-bodied truck, and the **M821** bridge transporter. The **M816** and **M819** were recovery vehicles.

To these models could be added extras such as winches, deep wading kits, cold weather kits, and so on. All these trucks retained the 'classic' American military truck appearance with the long bonnet, spartan soft-topped cab, and a large carrying area at the rear over doubled-up tyres on the rear axles.

Numerous variations on the above-mentioned models have appeared over the years, such as specialised bridging trucks and engineer equipment carriers. The cargo versions are often used as artillery tractors. Many remain in US armed forces service and with many other nations from South Korea to Panama and from Lebanon to Honduras. They will remain around for years to come but are scheduled to be replaced eventually by the 6 x 6 component of the projected Family of Medium Tactical Vehicles (FMTV).

M809 Series

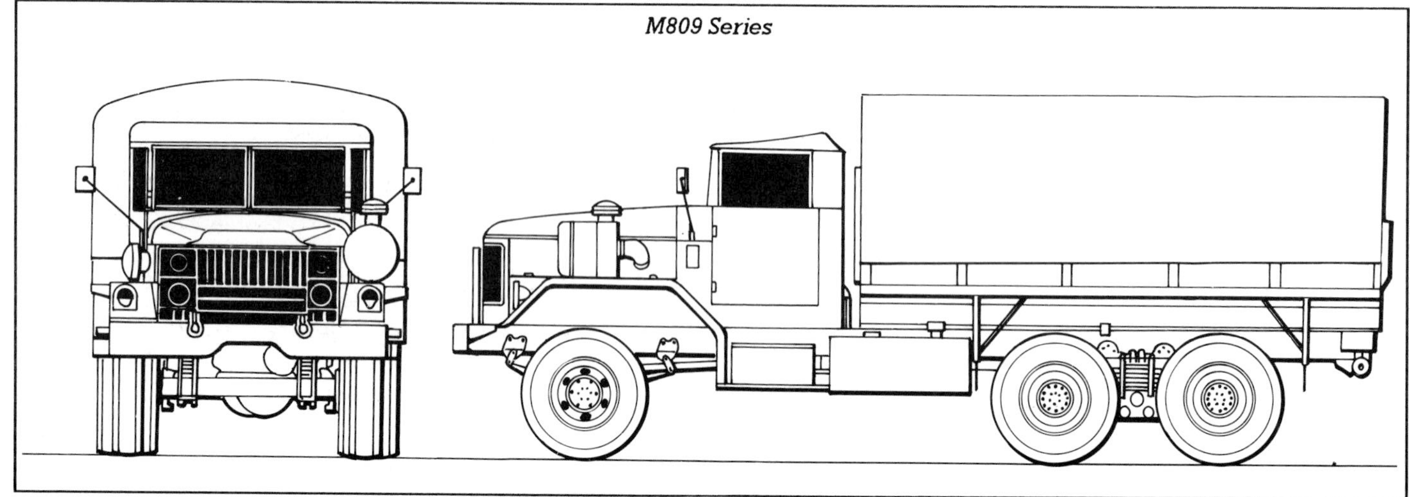

Specification

Role: general utility truck
Cab seating: 1 + 1 or 2
Configuration: 6 x 6
Weight: (empty) 9733 kg
Max load: 4535 kg
Length: 7.652 m
Width: 2.464 m
Height: 2.946 m
Ground clearance: 0.295 m
Track: 1.88 m/1.829 m
Wheelbase: 3.86 m + 1.37 m
Max speed: (road) 84 km/h
Fuel capacity: 295 litres
Fording: 0.76 m
Engine: Cummins NHC-250 14 litre 6-cylinder diesel
Power output: 240 hp/2100 rpm
Gearbox: manual, 5f, 1r
Clutch: single dry plate
Transfer box: 2-speed
Steering: power assisted
Turning circle: 25.5 m
Suspension: leaf springs, inverted at rear
Tyres: 11.00 x 20
Electrical system: 24 V

Variants: M813, M813A1, M814, M815, M816, M817, M818, M819, M820, M821

M809 5-ton truck in the classic general service form

M939 Truck Series

USA

The **M939** series was developed as early as 1970 as the result of a 'Product-Improved' programme to up-date the earlier M809 series of 5 ton trucks. The project was beset with delays and it was 1982 before the first units were delivered. The overall appearance of the M809 and **M939** remained much the same but the **M939** had many detail changes. These included an automatic transmission, an improved transfer case match to the transmission and air brakes. Other improvements were a better overall performance, the ability to wade up to 1.5 metres (with an add-on kit) and a cab with a true ability to seat three - earlier models could seat three only at a squeeze.

There were many other detail changes, including the ability to fit an Enhanced Mobility System (EMS), a central tyre inflation system which improves mobility over mud, sand and snow.

The **M939** series was produced in the usual wide array of M-number models (from **M923** to **M945** inclusive), most of which differed only in having a winch or not, or in wheelbase length.

There are standard cargo, long wheelbase cargo, dropside cargo, tippers, tractor trucks, wreckers and expansible bodies (for workshops, etc).

In 1986 production of the **M939** series was transferred from AM General to BMY (although AM continued in production for a while) with BMY making the **M939A2**, a version with a more powerful Cummins engine that also provides a greater range, reduced kerb weight, and the EMS tyre inflation system fitted as standard.

Production continues at Marysville, Ohio, in the full array of model types as before.

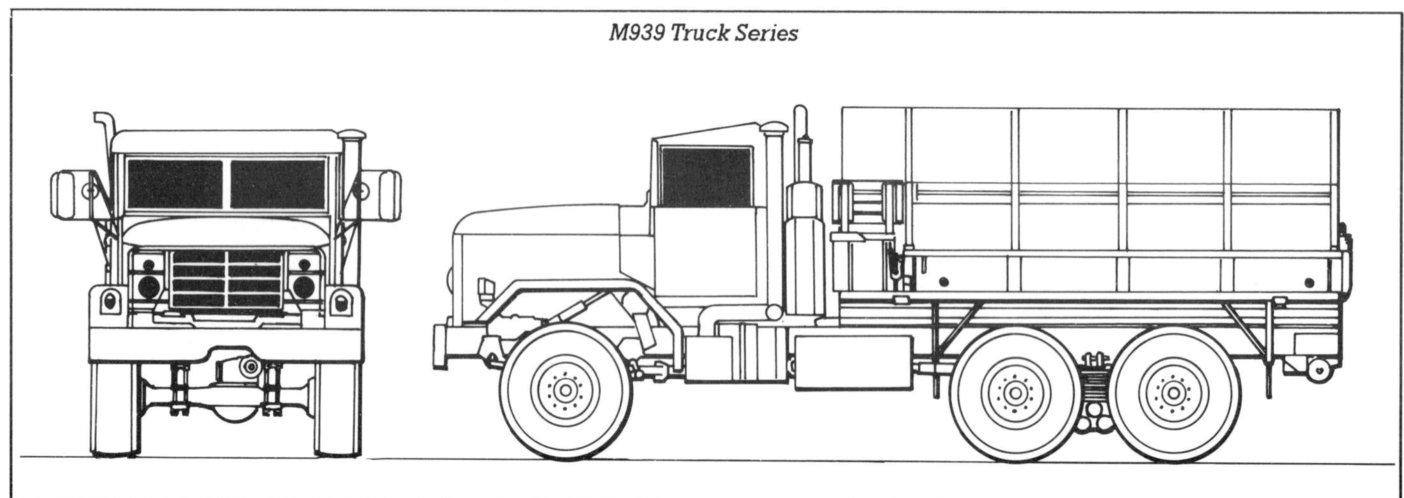

M939 Truck Series

Specification
Data for M923A2

Role: general utility truck
Cab seating: 1 + 2
Configuration: 6 x 6
Weight: (empty) 9947 kg
Max load: 4560 kg
Length: 7.886 m
Width: 2.47 m
Height: 3.07 m
Ground clearance: 0.33 m
Track: 1.981m/2.065 m
Wheelbase: 4.547 m
Max speed: (road) 86 km/h
Fuel capacity: 295 litres
Fording: 0.76 m
Engine: Cummins 6CTA8.3 8.3 litre 6-cylinder turbocharged diesel
Power output: 240 hp/2100 rpm
Gearbox: automatic, 5f, 1r
Clutch: single dry plate
Transfer box: 2-speed
Steering: hydraulic, power assisted
Turning circle: 25.5 m
Suspension: leaf springs, inverted at rear
Tyres: 11.00 x 20
Electrical system: 24 V

Variants: see text

M939 series truck towing 155 mm M198 howitzer

LMTV

USA

In 1991, Stewart & Stevenson of Sealy, Texas, were awarded a large-scale contract to manufacture the US Army's new Family of Medium Tactical vehicles (FMTV) with the intention that eventually all the existing (and ageing) medium trucks in the Army's inventory would be replaced by a modern and efficient design.

The FMTV is based on an Austrian truck, the Steyr 12 M 18, but considerably re-engineered to be available as the 4 x 4-2.5 ton Light Medium Tactical Vehicle (LMTV) and the 6 x 6-5 ton Medium Tactical Vehicle (MTV). Both models share over 90 per cent of components in common such as the cab, engine, drive train, tyres, wheels, front suspension, axles, etc, and involve many commercial components. The basic LMTV is the M1078 cargo while the 6 x 6 base is the M1083. Both basic models will have many variants, such as long wheelbase versions, van bodies, dump trucks, a 6 x 6 wrecker and a tractor truck, and special versions for low-altitude air drops. Some will be fitted with load handling cranes and others will have recovery winches. Both versions are being produced as bare chassis for special bodies to be added. Both base models use the same forward control cab which has features such as ease of maintenance and routine checking facilities. A machine gun mounting is provided over the cab. The driver is provided with power steering and a fully automatic transmission coupled to a high efficiency and low emission Caterpillar diesel.

Throughout the exercise the FMTV accent has been on reliability, low unit and running costs, and long term efficiency, all aspects well demonstrated during a gruelling series of selection trials which took place over a period of many months before selection of the Steyr design.

The FMTV family is destined to serve well into the 21st Century and is being offered for export sales in the Far East and elsewhere.

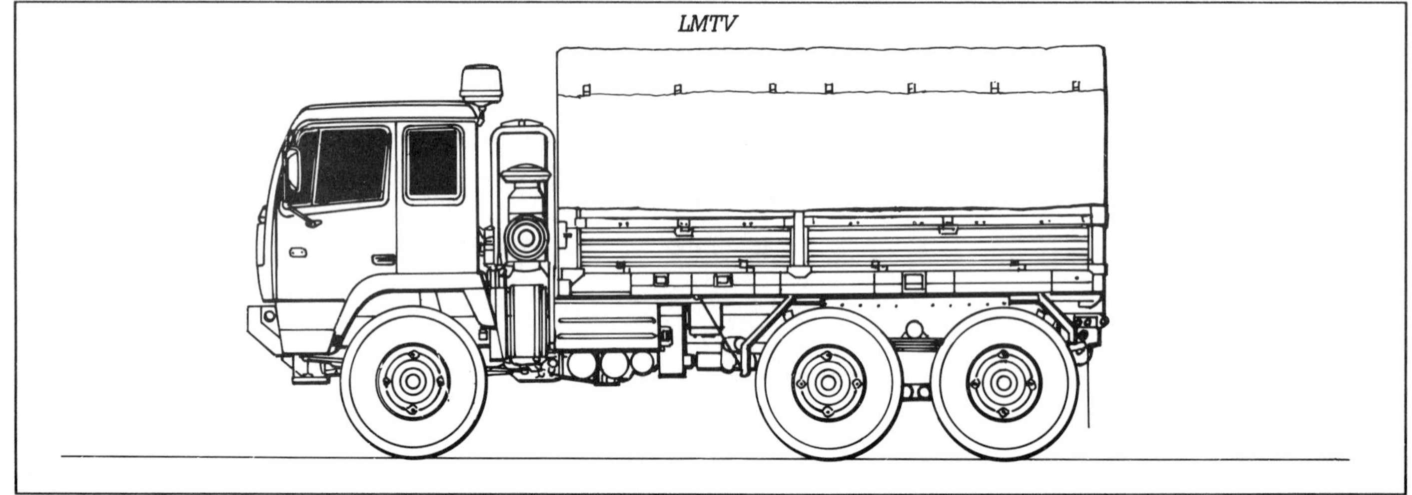

Specification

Model: LMTV/MTV
Role: utility/utility
Cab seating: 1 + 2/1 + 2
Configuration: 4 x 4/6 x 6
Weight: (empty) 7310 kg/8715 kg
Max load: 2268 kg/4536 kg
Length: 6.4065 m/6.9335 m
Width: 2.4 m2.4 m
Height: 3.1815 m/3.1873 m
Ground clearance: 0.564 m/0.564 m
Wheelbase: 3.9 m/4.1 m
Max speed: (road) 89 km/h/89 km/h
Fording: 0.923 m/0.923 m
Engine: Caterpillar 3115 ATAAC
Power output: 225 hp/290 hp
Gearbox: automatic 7f/1r
Transfer box: 2-speed /2-speed
Steering: power/power
Suspension: leaf springs/leaf springs
Tyres: 395 R 20/395 R 20
Electrical system: 12/24 V/12/24 V

Variants: see text

Factory finished LMTV ready for delivery

Oshkosh Mark 48 Series

USA

The MK 48 series of articulated trucks began life as a Lockheed design named the 'Twister', later developed into a commercial design known as the Dragon Wagon.

Following a licence agreement with Lockheed, the Oshkosh Truck Corporation developed the design into the DA series which, after the usual series of trials, was ordered by the US Marine Corps in 1983 as the MK 48 - 1433 vehicles were ordered.

There are four models in the MK 48 range. The **MK 48/14** is a flatbed truck equipped to carry standard logistics containers. The **MK 48/15** is a recovery vehicle equipped with a hydraulic crane and a heavy recovery winch. The **MK 48/16** is a shorter wheelbase truck tractor capable of pulling tank transporter semi-trailers, while the **MK58/17** is a cargo carrier with a hydraulic load handling crane and capable of carrying loads up to 18,144 kg on roads.

All models share the same articulated joint feature with the joint dividing the vehicle into front and rear modules. The joint is located behind the front pair of axles. In theory, the front module could be used with any of the other rear modules.

A self-recovery winch is a standard fitting while optional equipment includes sand tyres and a cold weather conversion kit. Mobility across country is understood to be excellent, even with full loads, but only the US Marine Corps purchased the MK 48 series (1433 units).

Oshkosh Mark 48 Series

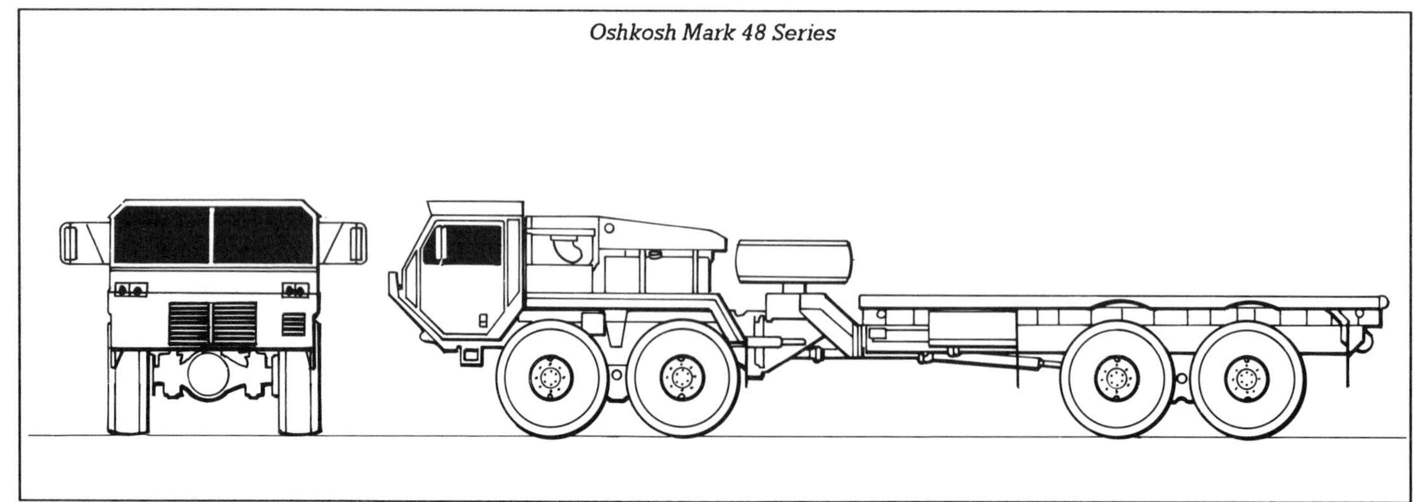

Specification
Data for MK 48/17

Role: heavy logistics truck
Cab seating: 1 + 1
Configuration: 8 x 8
Weight: (empty) 21,769 kg
Max load: 9072 kg
Length: 11.58 m
Width: 2.438 m
Height: 2.59 m
Ground clearance: approx 0.35 m
Track: 2 m
Wheelbase: 1.524 m + 6.579 m + 1.524 m
Max speed: (road) 84 km/h
Fuel capacity: 568 litres
Fording: 0.1.524 m
Engine: Detroit Diesel 8V-92TA 12 litre V8 diesel
Power output: 445 hp/2100 rpm
Gearbox: Allison automatic, 4f, 1r
Transfer box: 2-speed
Steering: hydraulic, power assisted
Turning circle: 23.4 m
Suspension: leaf springs and torque rods
Tyres: 16.00 x 21
Electrical system: 24 V

Variants: see text

Oshkosh MK 48/17 cargo truck

HEMTT

Development of the Oshkosh High Expanded Mobility Tactical Truck (**HEMTT**) series commenced during 1978 and a large scale order was placed by the US Army in 1981 - initial contracts totalled well over 7,400 units and follow-on funding has been provided for a further 4,536. The unit price was reduced by using commercially available components such as the axles, the automatic transmission, and a standard V8 diesel, but once in service the axles proved troublesome, producing into-service delays. Once these problems were overcome the **HEMTT** entered US Army service in large numbers.

The base model is the **M977** cargo truck provided with a small load handling crane behind the forward control cab.

The **M978** is a fuel servicing truck with a 9,500-litre capacity. The **M983** is a tractor truck for towing heavy semi-trailers capable of carrying tanks, while the **M984A1** is a recovery vehicle. The **M985** is another cargo truck, this time equipped with a heavy load handling crane at the rear; the **M985** is intended primarily to support Multiple Launch Rocket System (MLRS) units and is used in conjunction with a special cross-country trailer. To this range of basic models has been added a further variant with an extra axle added to give it a 10 x 10 configuration. This variant is equipped with a load-handling system capable of loading and unloading stores-carrying flatracks used for ammunition and other front-line combat supplies. It is understood that over 3,000 examples of these Palletized Loadhandling System (**PLS**) vehicles will be ordered by the US Army.

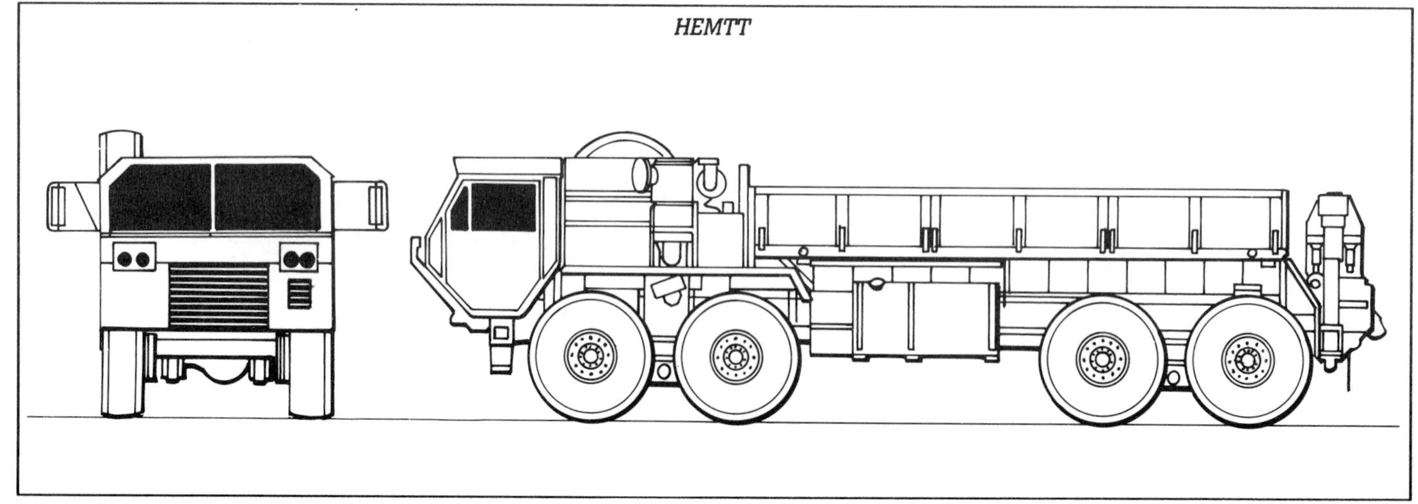
HEMTT

Specification
Data for M977

Role: heavy logistics truck
Cab seating: 1 + 1
Configuration: 8 x 8
Weight: (empty) 17,600 kg
Max load: 11,840 kg
Length: 10.173 m
Width: 2.438 m
Height: 2.565 m
Ground clearance: approx 0.35 m
Track: 1.977 m
Wheelbase: 5.334 m
Max speed: (road) 88 km/h
Fuel capacity: 589 litres
Fording: 0.76 m
Engine: Detroit Diesel 8V-92TA 12 litre V8 diesel
Power output: 445hp/2100 rpm
Gearbox: Allison automatic, 4f, 1r
Transfer box: 2-speed
Steering: hydraulic
Suspension: leaf springs and equalising beams
Tyres: 16.00 x 20
Electrical system: 24 V

Variants: see text

Oshkosh M978 fuel tanker, one of the trucks in the HEMTT series

Renault TRM 700-100T France

The French Army still retains many types of ageing tank transporters in service, most too old and/or light to handle with ease the loads imposed by the French Army's latest tank, the 53-tonne Leclerc.

Renault Vehicules Industriels (RVI) have therefore developed the **TRM 700-100T** tractor truck capable of towing loads up to 80 tonnes across country. Powered by a Renault (Mack) Type E9 700 hp turbocharged diesel coupled to an electronically- controlled seven-speed automatic transmission, the **TRM 700-100T** also has a hydraulic torque converter and a transfer box integral with the gearbox.

There is a roomy four-door crew cab based on that used by the Renault **TRM 10 000** truck (qv) which has seating for the driver and four passengers. The cab has all the usual heating and other provisions for the crew and even has provision for NBC equipment stowage. Behind the cab is space for two optional 15 tonne capacity hydraulic winches - another option is special wheels and tyres for use over soft terrain. Floodlights are provided on the cab roof to assist during night operations.

To date no special semi-trailer has been produced specifically for the **TRM 700-100T** so the prototype has been demonstrated towing several makes of semi-trailer. Extensive trials have been conducted since the vehicle first appeared in 1987 and a production order was expected by the beginning of 1991.

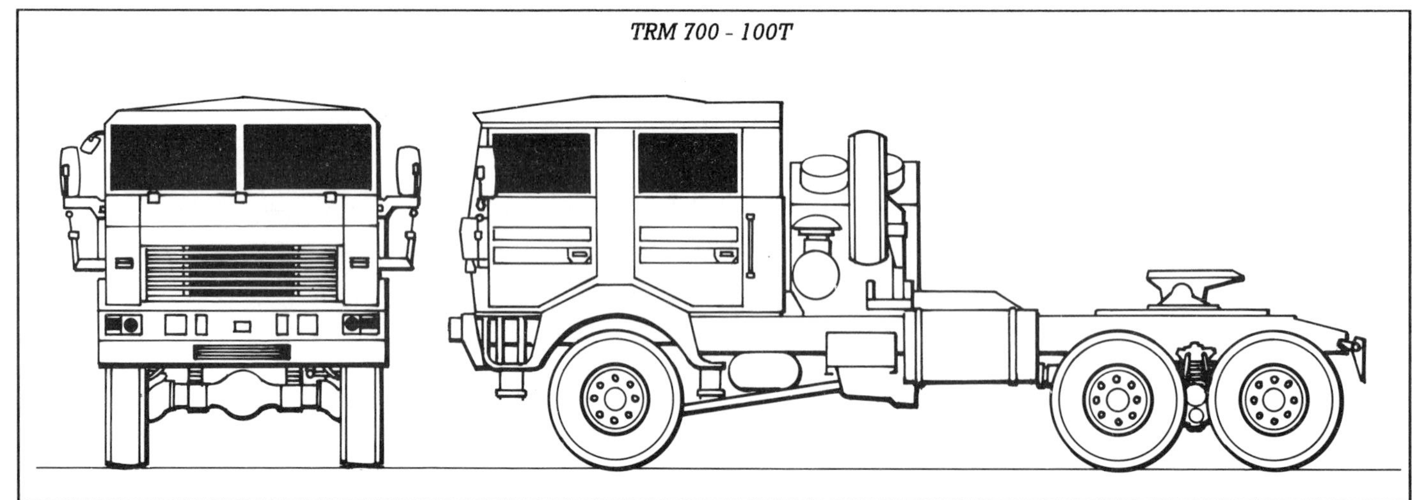
TRM 700 - 100T

Specification

Role: heavy tank transporter tractor truck
Cab seating: 1 + 4
Configuration: 6 x 6
Weight: (empty) 38,000 kg
Max load on 5th wheel: 23,000 kg
Length: 8.045 m
Width: 2.48 m
Height: 3.05 m
Ground clearance: 0.283 m
Track: 1.912 m/1.825 m
Wheelbase: 4.325 m + 1.35 m
Max speed: (road) 76 km/h
Fuel capacity: 720 litres
Fording: 0.75 m
Engine: RVI Type E9 16.4 litre V8 turbocharged diesel
Power output: 700 hp/2500 rpm
Gearbox: automatic, 7f, 1r
Transfer box: 2-speed
Steering: hydraulic power assisted
Turning circle: 23.2 m
Suspension: leaf springs, inverted at rear, and shock absorbers
Tyres: 13 x 22.5
Electrical system: 24 V

Variants: None - see text

Renault TRM 700-100 6 x 6 tractor truck

Faun FS 42.75/42 Germany

The **Faun FS 42.75/42** was designed to replace the earlier **Faun SLT 50-2** 'Elefant' tank transporters in service with the former West German Army.

Although the two vehicles are similar in many ways the **FS 42.75/42** has many improvements over the earlier model which dated its origins back to the Heavy Equipment Transporter 70 international project of the late 1960s. The later model, introduced in 1981 and intended to be a relatively low cost design, embodies experience gained since that project. This is noticeable in the transmission arrangement which combines a ZF torque converter with an automatic transmission to provide drive power to suit almost any permissible load and terrain conditions.

For steering the two front axles are used but only the front axle is driven. The **FS 42.75/42** is in service with the German Army where it is mainly used to tow Leopard 2 tanks, the remaining **SLT 50-2s** being retained to tow Leopard 1s. The two vehicles share a similar forward control cab, with seating for the driver and three passengers; a hatch with provision for a machine gun mounting is provided in the roof.

The cab also contains stowage for a number of German Army items such as tool boxes, weapon holders, signal flags and anti-skid chains. Behind the cab is a winch assembly housing a dual winch arrangement which is used for loading and unloading operations.

Numerous forms of optional equipment are available for use with this vehicle, including sand tyres, but the most involved factory-built option is a full 8 x 8 version, the **FS 42.75/48**.

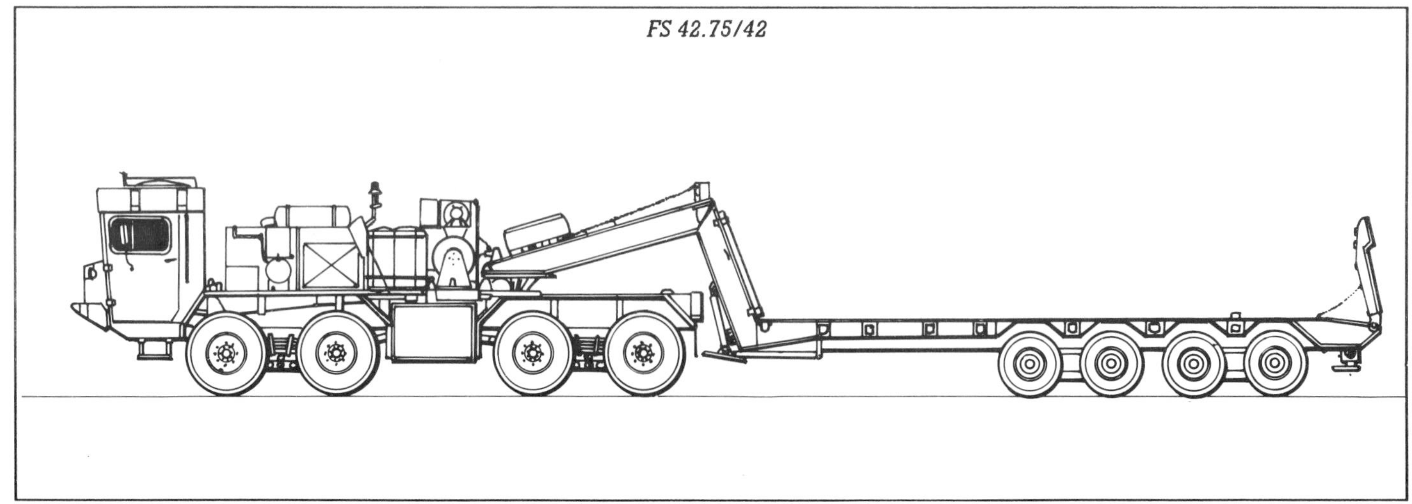

FS 42.75/42

Specification

Role: heavy tank transporter tractor truck
Cab seating: 1 + 3
Configuration: 8 x 6
Weight: (empty) 19,700 kg
Max load on 5th wheel: 20,000 kg
Length: 8.835 m
Width: 3.07 m
Height: 3.02 m
Ground clearance: approx 0.3 m

Track: 2.585 m/2.612 m
Wheelbase: 2 m + 2.7 m + 2 m
Max speed: (road) 72 km/h
Fuel capacity: 800 litres
Fording: 0.5 m
Engine: KHD 19 litre 12-cylinder diesel
Power output: 525 hp/2300 rpm
Gearbox: ZF torque converter with Ecosplit gearbox, 16f, 2r

Steering: ZF hydraulic
Turning circle: 22.4 m
Suspension: leaf springs and shock absorbers
Tyres: 18.00 x 22.5 XS
Electrical system: 24 V

Variants: SLT 50-2, FS 42.75/42, FS 42.75/48

Faun FS 42.75/42 8 x 6 tractor truck towing Leopard 2 MBT

Mercedes-Benz 4850A Tank Transporter Germany

The **4850 A** is the largest component in the Mercedes-Benz tank transporter range and differs from its close counterpart, the **4050 A** in having twin tyres on the rear axles in place of the twin or single sand tyres possible with the **4850 A**.

Both models are part of a tank transporter range that includes the 6 x 6 **3850 AS** and less powerful **2636 AS**.

The range shares many components in common, for instance all models have the same 18.2 litre V10 diesel engine, rated at 355 hp for the **2636 AS** and 500 hp for all other models.

The cab is virtually the same throughout, with seating for up to six passengers (four on a folding bench seat located on the rear cab wall) plus the driver, although this might be varied.

The range was developed for export, Pakistan taking about 100 examples of the **2636 AS**, and can thus be modified extensively to suit customer requirements. The types of loading winch can be varied as can options such as cab air conditioning, tool and other stowage, and the fuel tank capacity which can be varied between 400 and 1,000 litres on the 8 x 8 **4050 A** and **4850 A**. ZF or Allison transmissions can be installed on the 8 x 8 models.

For extended travel over sandy or other soft terrain a central tyre pressure regulation system can be provided when single sand tyres are fitted to the rear axles. Differential locks are provided on all axles.

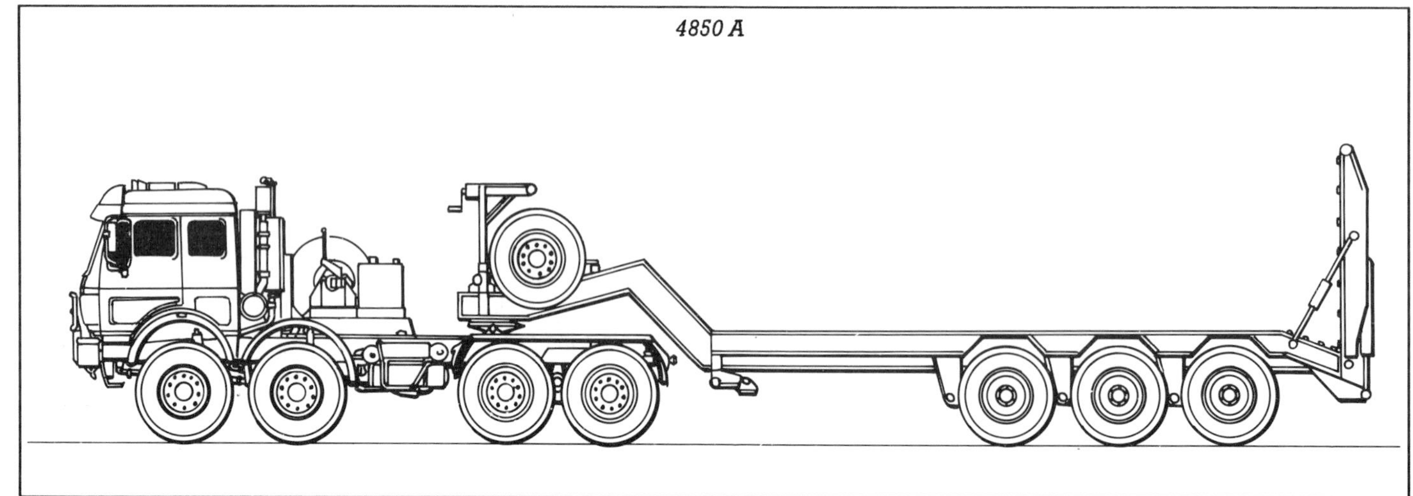
4850 A

Specification

Role: heavy tank transporter tractor truck
Cab seating: 1 + 6
Configuration: 8 x 8
Weight: (empty) 18,100 kg
Max load on 5th wheel: 31,000 kg
Length: 8.435 m
Width: 2.765 m
Height: 3.46 m
Ground clearance: 0.39 m
Track: 2.07 m/1.965 m

Wheelbase: 1.6 m + 2.935 m + 1.48 m
Max speed: (road) 90 km/h
Fuel capacity: 400 to 1000 litres
Fording: approx 0.8 m
Engine: Mercedes-Benz OM 423 LA 18.2 litre V10 diesel
Power output: 500 hp/2300 rpm
Gearbox: ZF torque converter or Allison automatic

Transfer box: 2-speed with automatic transmission
Steering: power
Turning circle: 22.5 m
Suspension: leaf springs with shock absorbers
Tyres: 24 R 21 or 14.00 x 20
Electrical system: 24 V

Variants: 4050 A

Mercedes-Benz 4850 A 8 x 8 tank transporter towing Leopard 2 MBT

IVECO 320.45 WTM

Italy

The first prototype of the **IVECO 320.45 WTM** was produced in 1978 in answer to an Italian Army requirement calling for a vehicle capable of towing a Leopard 1 (or similar) tank in off-road conditions. The resultant vehicle can tow tanks weighing up to 60 tonnes using a semi-trailer produced by Bartoletti.

The **320.45 WTM** uses a forward control cab with a soft top, although an optional hard top is available. Seating is limited to the driver and three passengers and the cab can be tilted forward for repairs and maintenance. For improved cross country performance the fifth wheel is fully articulated and a good towing capability is provided by the transmission's combination of a synchromesh gearbox, torque converter and a permanent 6 x 6 drive configuration.

For loading and unloading two 20 tonne capacity winches are located behind the cab. For use over sandy terrain a special sand version is produced with single 14.00 x 24 tyres on the front axle and single 24.00 x 20.5 tyres on the rear axles; the kerb weight of this version is reduced to 14,700 kg.

On both models a special high performance cooling system is provided for use when the engine is operating when stationary during prolonged loading and unloading operations.

Optional equipment includes a six-man cab, a towing hook for standard trailers, an auxiliary fuel tank, a front-mounted self-recovery winch, a fording kit for water obstacles up to 1.2 metres deep, and a hydrodynamic retarder.

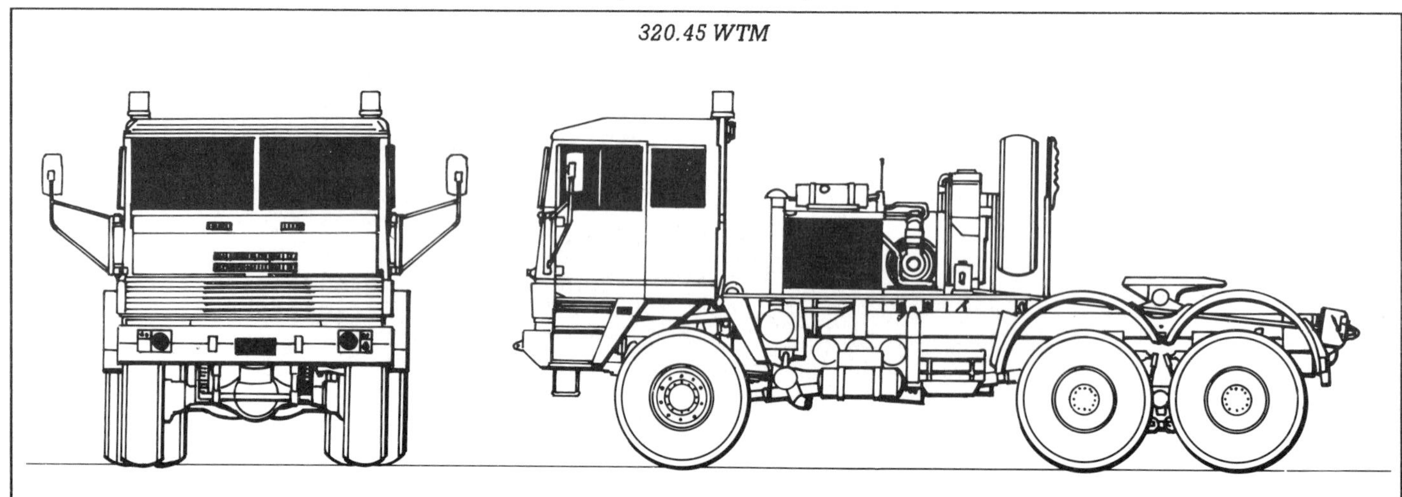
320.45 WTM

Specification

Role: heavy tank transporter
Cab seating: 1 + 3
Configuration: 6 x 6
Weight: (empty) 15,420 kg
Max load on 5th wheel: 22,000 kg
Length: 7.52 m
Width: 2.77 m
Height: 3.05 m
Ground clearance: 0.363 m
Track: 1.985 m/1.97 m

Wheelbase: 3.6 m + 1.38 m
Max speed: (road) 65 km/h
Fuel capacity: 500 litres
Fording: 0.85 m
Engine: FIAT 17.2 litre V8 turbocharged diesel
Power output: 450 hp/2400 rpm
Gearbox: synchromesh with torque converter, 8f, 1r
Transfer box: single-speed

Steering: powered
Turning circle: 19 m
Suspension: leaf springs
Tyres: front, 14.00 x 20
Electrical system: 24 V

Variants: see text

IVECO 320-45 WTM 6 x 6 tractor truck

MAZ-537

First observed during late 1964, the **MAZ-537** tank transporter tractor is closely related to the **MAZ-543** truck series (qv) and was developed in conjunction with the **MAZ- 535** heavy truck series; the **MAZ-537A** and **MAZ-537K** are 15 tonne cargo trucks, the latter also having a small crane.

The **MAZ-535** and **MAZ-537** share many components including the same 38.3 litre V12 diesel engine, also used by some Russian tanks (derated to 375 hp on the **MAZ-535**).

One typical Russian addition to the engine is a pre-heater to assist starting in cold climates and the cab is also well provided with heating. The maximum towed load of the **MAZ-537** is 15,000 kg which means that it can tow the latest generations of battle tanks only with some difficulty but it remains in widespread service with many nations, including Egypt, Finland and Syria.

Driving a fully-loaded **MAZ-537** is understood to be something of a task, even though there is power-assisted steering on the front four wheels; a central tyre inflation system is provided to provide better traction over soft ground or sand.

Variations of the **MAZ-537** are used to tow special semi-trailers containing the equipment required to support various weapon systems and heavy radar equipments; many of these special vehicles carry extra power generators behind the engine compartment.

It is understood that production of all the **MAZ-535** series of heavy trucks ceased at Minsk some time ago and a more modern design has been anticipated for some time.

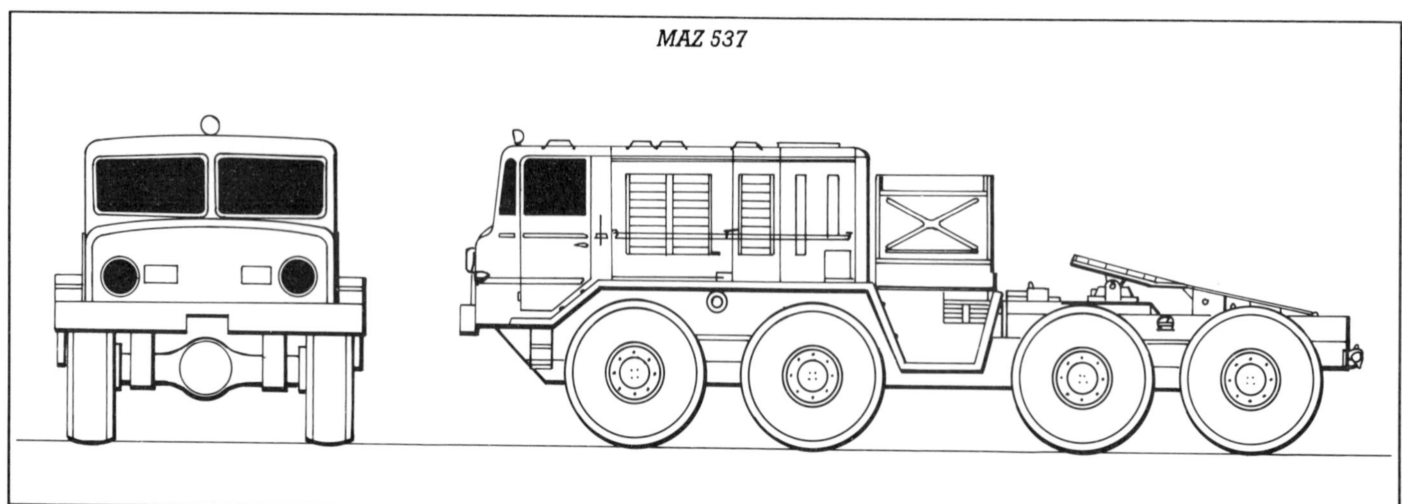

MAZ 537

Specification

Role: heavy tank transporter tractor truck
Cab seating: 1 + 3 or 4
Configuration: 8 x 8
Weight: (empty) 21,600 kg
Max load on 5th wheel: 22,000 kg
Length: 8.96 m
Width: 2.885 m
Height: 2.88 m
Ground clearance: 0.55 m
Track: 2.2 m
Wheelbase: 1.8 m + 2.65 m + 1.7 m
Max speed: (road) 55 to 60 m/h
Fuel capacity: 840 litres
Fording: 1.3 m
Engine: D12A-525 38.3 litre V12 diesel
Power output: 525 hp/2100 rpm
Gearbox: planetary, 3f, 1r
Clutch: single dry plate
Transfer box: 2-speed
Steering: hydraulic, screw and nut
Turning circle: approx 23 m
Suspension: independent lever torsion bar
Tyres: 18.00 x 24
Electrical system: 24 V

Variants: MAZ-543, MAZ-535, MAZ-537, MAZ-537E, MAZ-537G, MAZ- 537A, MAZ-537K

MAZ-537 8 x 8 tractor truck towing T-54/55 MBT

Unipower Commander

UK

Originally developed by Scammell (now Unipower Vehicles Limited) the **Commander** had its origins in a British Army requirement that envisaged main battle tanks weighing well over 60 tonnes.

Development began in 1976 but due to defence spending delays the production of a batch of 125 units for the British Army did not begin until 1983. The **Commander** remains part of the Unipower product range and the British Army use it to tow the **Challenger** 1 and 2 series of main battle tanks, the tanks the **Commander** was originally developed for - the old Thornycroft Antars previously in service were withdrawn from use.

Designed to tow loads of up to 65 tonnes, the **Commander** tows a special semi-trailer onto which tanks can be tail-loaded using a hydraulic 20 tonne capacity winch. A prominent bonnet houses the vehicle's Perkins (Rolls-Royce) CV 12 TCE V12 turbocharged diesel (similar to that used in the **Challenger 1** tank) which is coupled to an Allison automatic transmission incorporating a torque converter.

The cab (which may have air conditioning if required) has provision for up to three or four passengers and there is space for two bunks behind the front seats. Due to the front axle lock angle, the **Commander** is highly manoeuvrable and can negotiate a 'T' intersection with only 9.15 metres between the walls. Most of the 125 British Army **Commanders** are based in Belgium and West Germany with only a few located in the United Kingdom. Although the **Commander** is currently powered by a Perkins engine, other types may be installed in lieu - one of the prototypes used a Cummins KTA 600 diesel.

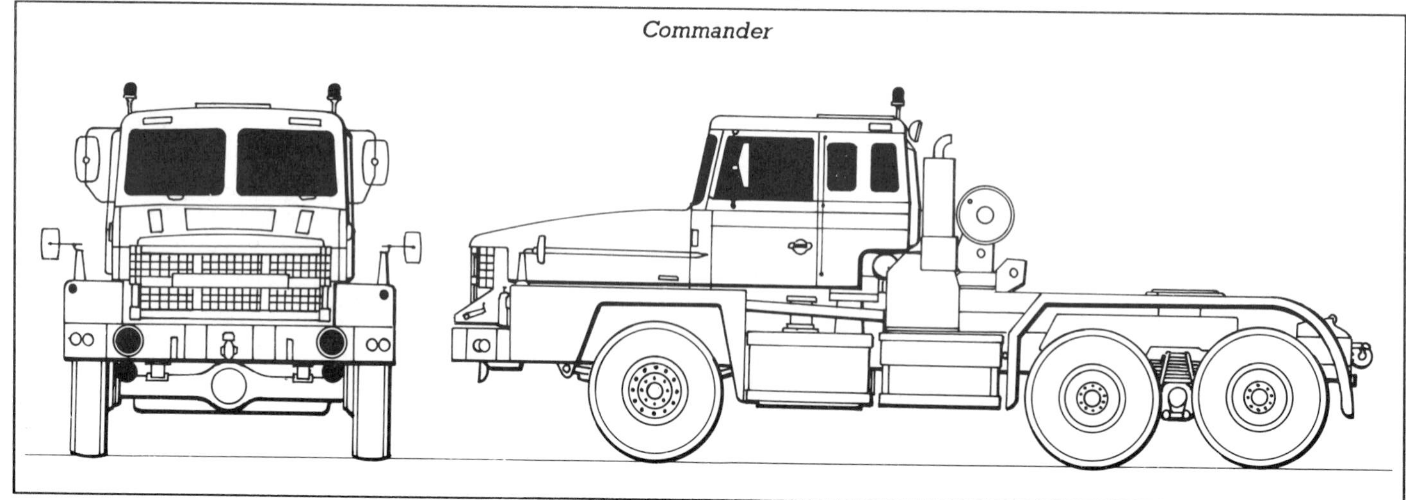

Commander

Specification

Role: heavy tank transporter tractor truck
Cab seating: 1 + 3 or 4
Configuration: 6 x 4
Weight: (empty) 19,920 kg
Max load on fifth wheel: 34,600 kg
Length: 9.01 m
Width: 3.25 m
Height: 3.5 m
Ground clearance: 0.45 m
Wheelbase: 5.03 m
Max speed: (road) 62 km/h
Fuel capacity: 817 litres
Fording: 0.76 m
Engine: Perkins (Rolls-Royce) CV-12 turbocharged diesel
Power output: 625 hp/2100 rpm
Gearbox: Allison automatic with torque converter, 6f, 1r
Steering: hydraulic
Turning circle: approx 24 m
Suspension: leaf springs and telescopic dampers
Tyres: 14.00 x 24
Electrical system: 24 V

Variants: None - see text

Unipower Commander tank transporter towing Chieftain MBT on semi-trailer

M1070 HET

USA

With the introduction of the **M1A1 Abrams** tank into service, the US Army's existing tank transporters were unable to carry the load. A contract was therefore awarded to the Oshkosh Truck Corporation to develop and manufacture a new heavy duty tank transporter which emerged as the **M1070 Heavy Equipment Transporter**; an order for an initial 522 units was originally placed, although it is expected that others will be required, and production commenced during July 1992.

The **M1070 HET** is a powerful tractor truck with an 8 x 8 drive configuration and advanced features such as an electronic engine control system to ensure maximum efficiency at all times, and an 'air ride' rear suspension to ensure all axles remain in contact with the ground at all times while smoothing out the worst round terrain shocks to the chassis frame. To assist traction further, across rough terrain, another standard feature is a central tyre inflation system (CTIS).

The engine remains the same as the earlier M911 (see next) but is uprated to deliver 500 hp and coupled to an automatic transmission. Another novel feature is the power-assisted steering system which synchronises the wheel movements on the front and rear axles to improve manoeuvrability in narrow confines.

Two 25 tonne loading winches are fitted as standard together with an auxiliary winch to handle cables and for general utility purposes. One improvement over earlier US Army tank transporters is that the cab has more space, for the crew of two and three passengers. The usual tank-carrying semi-trailer used with the **M1070 HET** is the M1000. Despite its bulk the **M1070 HET** can be air-transported in aircraft, although they have to be as large as a C-141 or C-5 to accommodate the tractor truck.

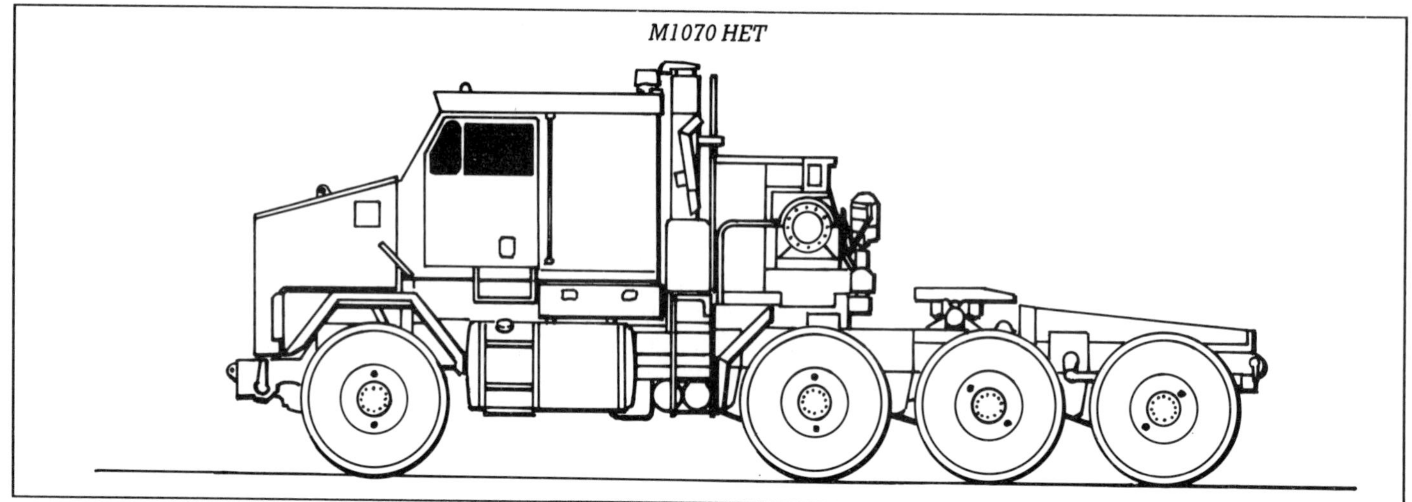
M1070 HET

Specification

Role: heavy tank transporter tractor truck
Cab seating: 1 + 3 or 4
Configuration: 8 x 8
Weight: (empty) 18,598 kg
Max load on fifth wheel: 21,325 kg
Length: 9.093 m
Width: 2.591 m
Height: 3.962 m
Wheelbase: 5.461 m

Max speed: (road) 72 km/h
Fuel capacity: 946 litres
Fording: 0.71 m
Engine: Detroit Diesel 8V-92TA-90 V8 diesel
Power output: 500 hp at 2100 rpm
Gearbox: Allison automatic 5f, 1r
Transfer box: Oshkosh 2-speed
Steering: hydraulic
Turning circle: 22.2 m

Suspension: front, springs and hydraulic shock absorbers; rear, air ride
Tyres: 16.00 x 20
Electrical system: 24 V

Variants: see text

Oshkosh M1070 Heavy Equipment Transporter (HET)

M911

USA

In 1976 the US Army issued a highly detailed set of requirements for a new tank transporter tractor truck with low cost and a proven commercial background being key points. These points arose from experience with the then-in-service **M746** tractor truck which proved to be expensive to maintain and operate. The resultant contract for 747 units, designated the **M911**, went to Oshkosh who based their submission on their F2365 commercial truck.

Production of the **M911** commenced during 1977. The **M911** has an unusual feature for such a vehicle in that the front axle of the rear three is an air-suspended pusher axle only and can be raised when not required; when lowered it decreases the fifth wheel load on the other two axles.

The Detroit Diesel V8 engine is coupled to an Allison automatic transmission and a torque converter is provided. Tanks are loaded onto the towed semi-trailer (usually the 60 ton M747) using two 20.4 tonne winches located behind the cab.

Following the completion of the US Army order an anticipated option for a further 445 units was not exercised so Oshkosh marketed the basic **M911** as their **Heavy Equipment Transporter (HET)** and were rewarded with an order for 12 from Thailand.

At one time the **M911/HET** was available with a wide range of extras such as an oscillating fifth wheel, extra electrical connections for deck lights etc, a tyre inflation hose, and many others, some of which are employed by the US Army.

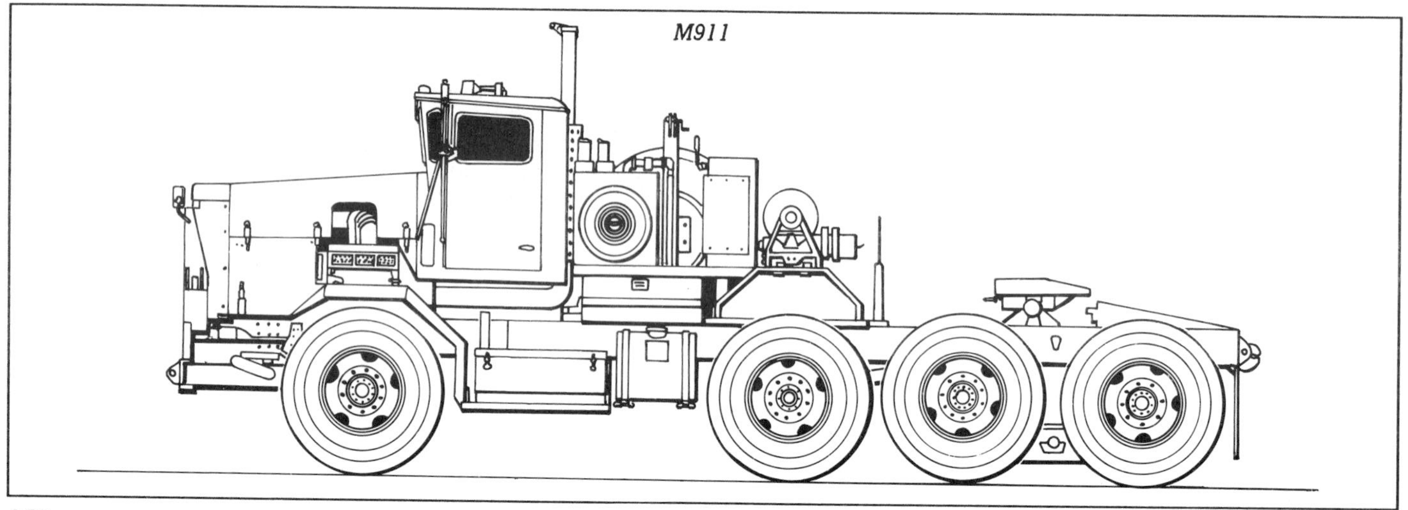

M911

Specification

Role: heavy tank transporter tractor truck
Cab seating: 1 + 2
Configuration: 6 x 6
Weight: (empty) 18,144 kg
Max load on fifth wheel: 20,866 kg
Length: 9.373 m
Width: 2.438 m
Height: 3.4 m
Ground clearance: 0.4 m
Wheelbase: 5.207 m + 1.524 m
Max speed: (road) 72 km/h
Fuel capacity: 757 litres
Fording: 0.71 m
Engine: Detroit Diesel 8V-92TA-90 V8 diesel
Power output: 450 hp/2100 rpm
Gearbox: Allison automatic 5f, 1r
Transfer box: single-speed
Steering: hydraulic
Turning circle: 29.5 m
Suspension: front, semi-elliptic springs; rear, springs and equalising beam
Tyres: 14.00 x 24
Electrical system: 24 V

Variants: see text

Oshkosh M911 Heavy Equipment Transporter (HET)

Bv 206 Series

Sweden

Development of the **Bv 206** all-terrain articulated tracked carrier began in 1974. Three batches of trials vehicles were delivered between 1976 and 1978 and the first production examples were delivered to the Swedish Defence Administration in 1980. Since then the **Bv 206** has been produced in thousands by Hagglunds and is in service all around the world.

The **Bv 206** in its basic carrier form is a twin-unit articulated tracked vehicle that can carry up to 17 troops or 2250 kg of supplies (6 troops or 630 kg in the front unit, 11 troops or 1620 kg in the rear unit). Normally both front and rear units are fully enclosed but for some applications the rear unit can vary considerably and in some cases is left fully open, such as for a mortar carrier, or can accommodate a variety of 'swop bodies'. The engine, originally a Ford V6 petrol unit but now a Mercedes-Benz diesel, is in the front unit together with the automatic transmission. Connection to the rear unit is made via an articulated joint which is also used for steering. Most bodies make extensive use of light plastic-based materials but the chassis uses light alloys. Variants of the basic **Bv 206** abound. It is used as a light artillery tractor, an ambulance, a communication or command post, to carry various anti-tank weapons such as the Bofors BILL or TOW, for ground-to-air missile systems such as the Bofors RBS 90, and even to carry radar systems. A light armoured version has been developed.

The **Bv 206** is widely used, especially by the Swedish armed forces, the US Army (who have developed a desert version), the British Armed Forces, and the German Army (who use only diesel-engined versions). The type has been licence-produced in Chile.

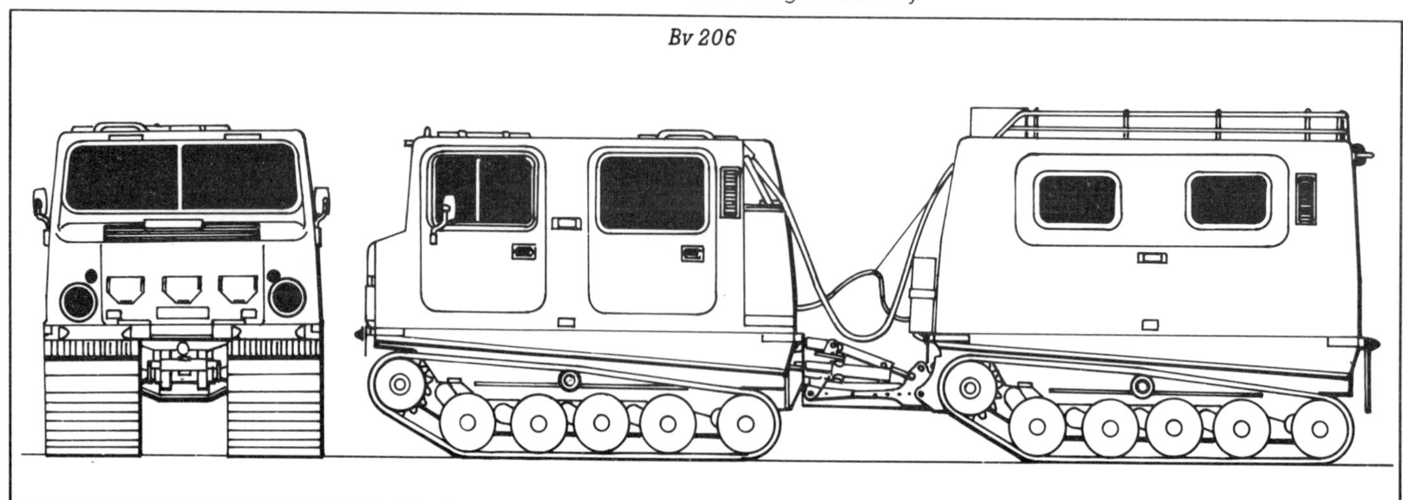
Bv 206

Specification

Role: general purpose all-terrain carrier
Cab seating: 1 + up to 16
Weight: (empty) 4380 kg
Max load: 2250 kg
Length: 6.89 m
Width: 1.85 m
Height: 2.4 m
Ground clearance: 0.35 m
Track width: 620 mm
Max speed: (road) 50 km/h
Fuel capacity: 160 litres
Fording: amphibious
Engine: Mercedes-Benz 3 litre 6 cylinder diesel
Power output: 136 hp/4600 rpm
Gearbox: automatic, 4f, 1r
Steering: hydrostatic
Turning circle: 16 m
Suspension: trailing arms and rubber tension springs
Electrical system: 24 V

Variants: see text

Bv 206 tracked all-terrain transporter

MT-S Tracked Transporter Former Soviet Union

The **MT-S** medium tracked transporter is employed mainly for forward area supply duties or to carry combat engineer equipment in remote areas where roads are scarce. It is one of the latest of a long line of similar tracked carriers produced within the USSR and first appeared during the early 1980s. Since then the **MT-S** has replaced many of the earlier Russian Army tracked carriers such as the **ATS-59** and **AT-T** but its present production status is uncertain, and it is apparently used only by Eastern Bloc armed forces and some Russian civilian agencies.

The basic **MT-S** is derived from the chassis and running gear of the 152 mm 2S3 (S-152) self-propelled howitzer. The layout has the driver seated at the left front with the engine located centrally behind him.

Although it has yet to be confirmed, this engine is understood to be the same as that used in the **MT-T** (qv) and is based on a T-72 tank engine.

A small cabin behind the driver can seat up to three passengers. The main load-carrying area is to the rear and is normally covered by a canvas tilt; a flatbed version may be used to carry shelter bodies. A towing hook at the rear can be used to tow light artillery pieces. A small snow plough or dozer blade can be fitted to the front of the vehicle for obstacle clearing. The same basic chassis and running gear is used on the **GMZ** tracked minelayer and a similar chassis is employed as a carrier for parts of the SA-11 (Gadfly) surface-to-air missile system, including some of the associated radars. The data provided in the specifications table should be regarded as provisional.

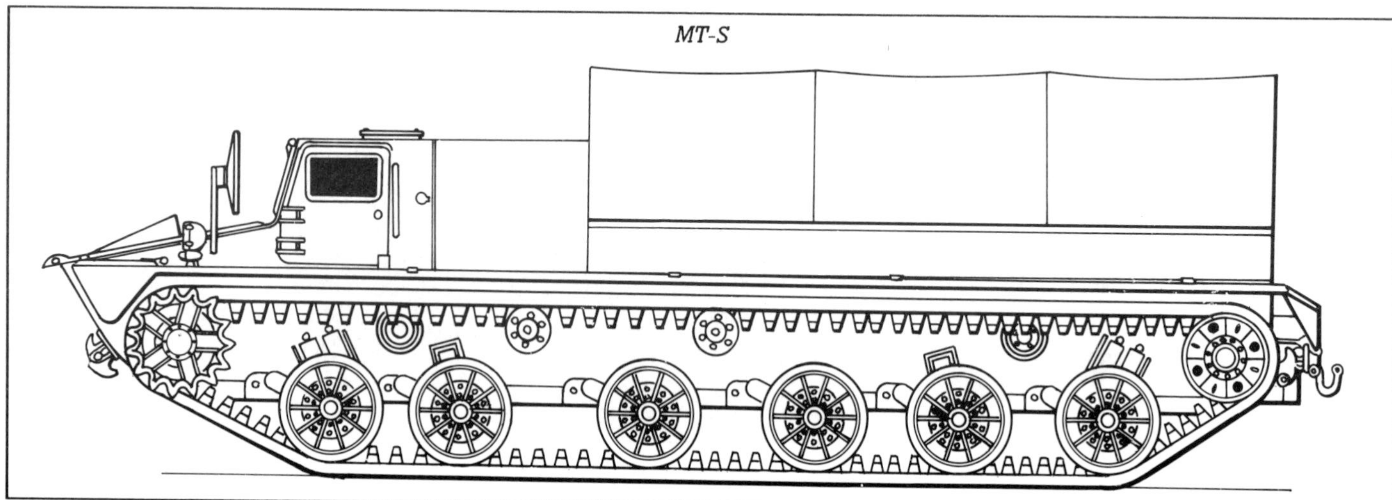
MT-S

Specification

Role: medium tracked transporter
Cab seating: 1 + 3
Weight: (empty) 23,500 kg
Max load: 10,200 kg
Length: 7.8 m
Width: 3.34 m
Height: 1.846 m
Ground clearance: 0.445 m
Track width: (centre to centre) 2.752 m

Max speed: (road) approx 65 km/h
Fuel capacity: 850 litres
Fording: 1.5 m
Engine: V12 diesel
Power output: 710 hp/? rpm
Turning circle: pivot on spot
Suspension: torsion bar
Electrical system: 24 V

Variants: see text

A rare photograph of the MT-S equipped with combat engineer equipment

M548

USA

The tracked cargo carrier that was to become the **M548** began life as a carrier for a radar system that did not enter production. That was in 1960 but by 1964 a revised version based on the running gear of the **M113A1** armoured personnel carrier was developed and was in production by 1966. It is still in production by the FMC Corporation in a multitude of forms.

The basic version of the **M548** has the crew cab and engine set well forward with the load area to the rear. The cab usually has a soft top and provision for some form of machine gun mounting. The drop sides and the tailgate for the load area can be removed to allow shelters for various communications or electronics systems to be installed - many **M548s** are used in this role and for nothing else.

One variant, the **M1015**, has been specifically developed for the electronic shelter carrying role. Other variants of the basic **M548A1** (the latest production version with a revised suspension) include the **M667/M668** launch and carrier vehicles for the Lance tactical missile system, the **M548GA1**, used by the German Army to carry and launch their MiWS scatterable mine system, the **M730**carrying four Chaparral surface-to-air missiles, and the support vehicles used by the British Army to support their Tracked Rapier air defence missile system.

Many other variants have been developed to the 'one off' stage and got no further. These included recovery vehicles, lightweight artillery rocket systems, and various 'stretched' versions with extra road wheels and more power. The **M548** series is now widely used by many nations outside the USA, including Australia, Canada, Israel, Switzerland and many others. Many of the user nations have introduced their own modifications and 'fits'.

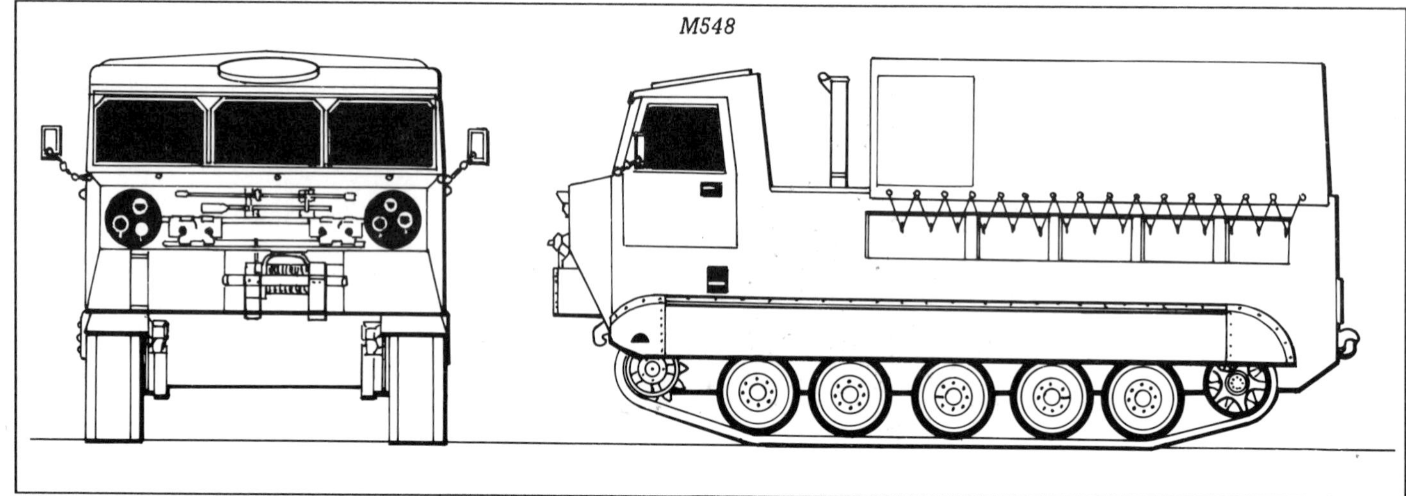
M548

Specification

Role: tracked cargo carrier
Cab seating: 1 + 3
Weight: (empty) 7440 kg
Max load: 5443 kg
Length: 5.892 m
Width: 2.69 m
Height: 2.71 m
Ground clearance: 0.43 m
Track width: 381 mm
Max speed: (road) 64 km/h
Fuel capacity: 397 litres
Fording: 1 m
Engine: GMC 6V-53 6-cylinder diesel
Power output: 215 hp/2800 rpm
Transmission: Allison automatic, 6f, 2r
Turning circle: pivot on spot
Suspension: torsion bar
Electrical system: 24 V

Variants: M548A1, M548GA1, M1015, M667/M668, M730

M1015 tracked carrier laden with radar equipment

Glossary

ACMAT	Ateliers de Construction Mecanique de l'Atlantique
ADE	Atlantis Diesel Engines
AM	American Motors
AWD	All Wheel Drive
BMY	Bowen-McLaughlin-York
CIS	Commonwealth of Independent States
CTIS	Central Tyre Inflation System
CUCV	Commercial Utility Cargo Vehicle
EMS	Enhanced Mobility System
f	forward
FMC	Food Machinery Corporation
FMTV	Family of Medium Tactical Vehicles
GB	Great Britain
GM	General Motors
hp	horsepower
HEMTT	Heavy Expanded Mobility Tactical Truck
HET	Heavy Equipment Transport
HMMWV	High Mobility Medium Wheeled Vehicle
HMRT	Heavy Material Recovery Team
IVECO	International Vehicle Corporation
JRA	Jaguar Rover Australia
LMTV	Light Medium Tactical Vehicle
MILAN	Missile d'Infantrie Anti-char
MiWS	Minenwurf System
MMV	Multi-Mission Vehicle
MLRS	Multiple Launch Rocket System
MTV	Medium Tactical Vehicle
PFM	Pont Flotant Motorise
r	reverse
RAF	Royal Air Force
rpm	revolutions per minute
SAMIL	South African Military
SAS	Special Air Service
TOW	Tube-launched, Optically-aimed, Wire-guided
Unimog	Universal Motor Gerat
UMM	Uniao Metalo Mecanica
UK	United Kingdom
USA	United States of America
VLRA	Vehicule Leger de Reconnaissance et d'Appui
VLTT	Vehicle Leger de Tout Terrain
ZF	Zahnradfabrik Friedrichshafen